Weber's Art of the Grill

recipes for outdoor living

Weber's
Art of the

Grill

recipes for outdoor living

FOREWORD
Mike Kempster, Sr.

TEXT AND RECIPE DEVELOPMENT
Jamie Purviance

PHOTOGRAPHS
Tim Turner

CHRONICLE BOOKS • SAN FRANCISCO

EDITORIAL TEAM:
Managing Editor: Ken Winchester
Writer: Jamie Purviance
Photographer: Tim Turner
Art Director: Robin Weiss
Design Assistant: Deborah Tibbetts
Food Stylist: Lynn Gagné
Assistant Food Stylist: Vanessa Dubiel
Prop Stylist: Renée L. Miller
Photo Assistants: Rod LaFleur,
Donald Bartkowiak
Copy Editor: Sharon Silva
Illustrator: Dick Cole
Cover Design: Bob Aufuldish
Contributing Editor: Sandra S. McRae
Contributors: Evan Elliot, Lois Hlavac,
    Jon King, Susan Lamb Parenti
Index: Nancy Mulvany

Produced by
ROUND MOUNTAIN MEDIA:
President: Susan Maruyama

WEBER–STEPHEN PRODUCTS CO.:
Executive Vice President: Mike Kempster, Sr.
Director of Consumer Affairs: Betty Hughes
Director of Marketing: Christina Schroeder

PRODUCTION:
St. Remy Multimedia

Printed in Canada

Library of Congress
Cataloging-in-Publication Data:

Weber's Art of the Grill/foreword by Mike
Kempster, Sr.; text by Jamie Purviance.
            p.   cm.
        ISBN 0-8118-2419-5
        1. Barbecue cookery.
        I. Weber (Firm)
    TX840.B3W35   1999
    641.5'784–dc21 98-32290
    CIP

10 9 8 7 6 5

Chronicle Books LLC
85 Second Street
San Francisco, California 94105

Distributed in Canada by Raincoast Books
9050 Shaughnessy Street
Vancouver, British Columbia V6P 6E5

WEB SITES:
www.weberbbq.com
www.chroniclebooks.com

contents

foreword

At Weber®, grilling is not just a pastime, it's a passion. The flames of this passion began as a spark in 1952 when George Stephen fashioned the first Weber Kettle Grill out of two buoy halves. George's covered grill was an instant hit with cooks across the country, and the kettle's unique shape quickly became a cultural icon.

Since then, we've been grilling in backyards around the country. Over the years our products have evolved from the simple to the sublime, from the original Weber Kettle to the masterfully crafted Summit® Gas Barbecue.

Along the way, America's tastes have evolved, too. It used to be that having a cookout meant it was a summer weekend, when you threw steaks or burgers and maybe some corn or potatoes on a grill. Now we grill year-round, even on weekdays. We grill entire menus, from casual to gourmet, from appetizers to dessert (yes, dessert!). In fact, the grill has become an extension of the kitchen, as indispensable as a blender or sauté pan—we might use it just to enhance the texture of a certain ingredient or to add a more robust flavor to a recipe. Looking back, I think the Weber Grill evolved from a well-thought-out backyard enhancement to an entertainment hub because grilling itself has become more than a cooking method. Today, it's an expression of lifestyle.

Two years ago, we set out to create a cookbook worthy of being paired with our top-of-the-line Summit Gas Barbecue.

We gathered a team of experts, and with tongs and spatulas in hand, they went to work developing, testing, and perfecting recipes for this book. We told them we wanted more than just another collection of appealing grilled dishes. We wanted extraordinary flavors that would surprise and delight your guests and family. We wanted to inspire you with photos as luscious as the food itself. And we wanted to provide special techniques and foolproof instructions that would make you a backyard hero.

In the process, we discovered grilling as an art form. And we soon realized that the recipes were so exceptional and the flavors so amazing that we had to make it available to anyone with a passion for grilling.

The tricks and techniques we've included here will help you serve up food that rivals the best restaurants. You can follow the directions to the letter and get great results, or use them as a great base for jumping off and doing your own thing. Either way, it is our sincerest hope that this book helps fulfill *your* passion for fabulous food.

Enjoy,

Mike Kempster, Sr.
Executive Vice President
Weber-Stephen Products Co.

introduction

We used to think of grilling primarily as cooking backyard basics for a crowd, but today our traditions have meshed with cuisines around the world to create a virtually limitless range of possibilities. While Americans show no signs of giving up the unparalleled satisfaction of a cheeseburger with all the fixings, or anything as fundamental to a good barbecue as baked beans, international flavors influence what we grill more than ever before. So for this book, we started with the recipes and cooking techniques that define the spirit of an all-American, down-home barbecue. A succulent pulled pork sandwich from the Carolinas, cedar-planked salmon from the Pacific northwest, and hickory-smoked turkey for Thanksgiving or any special occasion are just some of what we chose to represent America's original best. Along the way we have shared essential insider tips such as how to grill thick steaks so the center drips with precious juices while the surface carries the lightly charred and smoky character that only a grill can achieve. To accompany these classic recipes, we developed a collection of delicious, traditional side dishes, salads, and desserts that will round out whatever type of meal you prefer.

We have also included several authentic international recipes that have made themselves at home in America's backyard. Indonesian satay, Greek lamb chops with tzatziki, and Jamaican jerk chicken are just a few examples of what grillers around the globe have taught us. In dozens of other recipes in this book, we incorporated particular flavors or methods from nations near and far and used them to embellish American standards. For instance, we borrowed the Mexican tradition of roasting tomatillos and hot chile peppers on a searing grill to make the base of a vibrant sauce, which we serve with grilled pork chops. We looked to China for a subtly sweet and aromatic hoisin glaze with which to cook baby back ribs. Inspired by the soulful tastes of the Caribbean, we mixed rum, lime juice, and mangoes with other exotic seasonings to give grilled swordfish steaks a sultry character.

As you try the recipes in this book, remember that grilling remains simple. The variables are what make every experience uniquely gratifying. The recipes you choose, the type of grill you use, the weather outside, the people you invite---and certainly your frame of mind---all make a difference. My advice is to relax. Relish the chance to cook in the open air and serve food with the incomparable effects of sear and smoke. The possibilities have never been greater.

Good grilling,

Jamie Purviance

Writer and Recipe Developer

Grilling as an art form depends largely on controlling the fire, getting the seasonings just right, and mastering a few special techniques. First and foremost, the skilled griller must decide whether to use direct or indirect heat. In this chapter we explain why the decision is so critical and how to make the call yourself.

The next step is to preheat the grill on high for about ten minutes or until the temperature reaches 500–550°F. Then brush the cooking grate clean with a brass grill brush. For great grill marks

essentials

and to make sure food doesn't stick, you can lightly oil the cooking grate just before placing the food on it.

Another secret is to keep the cover on so the heat circulates evenly and the grill can impart more of that fabulous smoky flavor we love.

Next come the gadgets. There's no need to go wild and buy every one under the sun; consult the list on page 17 to build a small but effective collection.

All the recipes in this book were developed for and tested on Weber Summit® Gas Barbecues. You should have great success with these recipes even if you're not cooking on a Summit, but keep in mind that variables such as the wind and outside temperature, the size and shape of your ingredients and, most important, the grill you are using will affect cooking times. Get to know your own set of circumstances and let experience be your guide. Let's grill!

Washington

Local Indian tribes perfected the art of skewering salmon fillets on racks built of cedar, then grilling them over a fire of driftwood. Grilling is still preferred over barbecue, but the list of fish has grown dramatically. Lemon juice, butter, and fresh herbs make a tried-and-true basting mixture.

California's Central Coast

A holdover from the spring roundups at huge Mexican ranches that covered the region, Santa Maria-style tri-tip barbecue features beef that is seasoned with garlic, paprika, salt, and pepper and slow-cooked over red oak. It is traditionally accompanied by pinquito beans, salsa, and garlic bread.

Southwest

Fajitas are hot here, where Mexican, Californian, and Texan influences converge. Chiles, avocadoes, and other fresh produce create more of a blend of flavors than a contest of heat.

grilling traditions in the u.s.a.

Most of us use the terms grilling and barbecuing interchangeably, though aficionados believe the two should never be confused. Strictly speaking, grilling refers to medium- to high-heat cooking done directly over flames. Authentic barbecuing refers to low-heat cooking done indirectly over flames, usually with the addition of smoldering wood to flavor the food. To make matters a bit more interesting, regional styles of grilling and barbecuing can be very distinct. The preferred types of meat or sauce become topics that locals will argue over, insisting that their style is the only true form.

Kansas City, Missouri

With more barbecue restaurants than anywhere else in the country, this city is arguably Barbecue Capital of the U.S.A. Any type of meat is fair game for the barbecue, although pork and beef (especially ribs) rate high. The meat is seasoned with a rub or marinade, cooked over hickory, and served with a spicy tomato-and-molasses-based sauce.

Chicago, Illinois

Home of the U.S. meat-packing industry and the birthplace of Weber Grills, Chicago is where steak reigns supreme. At legendary steakhouses, aged prime beef is grilled over searing heat and served with fat fries and maybe a salad. When the meat is first-rate, there's little need for sauce.

New England

Yankee simplicity is epitomized by tossing clams, mussels, shrimp, and lobsters on the grill with little or no fuss. A few grilled vegetables, some steamed potatoes, perhaps some drawn butter, and dinner is ready. Fresh salt air is the traditional seasoning.

North Carolina

The essential ingredient here is pork, which is pit-cooked and served with a vinegar-based sauce. In the western part of the state, pork shoulder is popular and tomato or ketchup makes its way into the sauce. In eastern North Carolina, the whole hog is cooked and ketchup is a dirty word when it comes to sauce. Either way, the meat is piled on a soft white bun and accompanied with a side of slaw. And don't forget their legendary baked beans.

Texas

Beef, especially brisket, is the entrée of honor, and if smoke is involved, it's mesquite. Showing the influence from south of the border, they often break out the chiles and limes for Texan marinades, tenderizing the tougher cuts. Chile rubs are standard here, too—the hotter the better.

Memphis, Tennessee

Whether you like your pork ribs "dry" (prepared with a rub), "wet" (slathered with sauce), or with a little "shake on the side" (served with extra dry rub for those who can't get enough), you'll find a cure for the blues in Memphis. If a sauce is served, it's a spicy-sweet tomato-based blend. Add a heap of coleslaw and a mess of corn—and plenty of napkins—and you've got a meal fit for Elvis.

To grill by the Direct Method on a gas grill, preheat the grill with all burners on High. Place food directly above the heat in the center of the cooking grate, then adjust all burners to the temperature noted in the recipe.

direct cooking

The Direct Method is similar to broiling. Food is cooked directly over the heat source. For even cooking, food should be turned once halfway through the grilling time. The Direct Method is recommended for steaks, chops, kabobs, sausages, and other foods that take less than 25 minutes to cook.

Direct cooking also helps sear in juices on larger cuts of meat for maximum flavor and moistness. Simply sear meats on direct heat on each side, then finish grilling by the Indirect Method.

To grill by the Direct Method on a charcoal grill, spread hot coals evenly across the charcoal grate and place food in the center of the cooking grate.

To grill by the Indirect Method on a gas grill, preheat the grill with all burners on High. Then adjust the burners on each side of the food to the temperature noted in the recipe, and turn off the burner(s) directly below the food. For best results, place roasts, poultry, or large cuts of meat on a roasting rack set inside a disposable heavy-gauge foil pan. For longer cooking times, add water to the drip pan to keep drippings from burning.

indirect cooking

The Indirect Method is similar to roasting. Charcoal briquets are set on each side of the food and gas burners are lit on each side of the food but not directly beneath it. Heat rises, reflects off the lid and inside surfaces of the grill, and slowly cooks the food evenly on all sides. The circulating heat works much like a convection oven, so there's no need to turn the food. The Indirect Method is recommended for roasts, ribs, chickens, turkeys, and other large cuts of meat. Whether you're cooking by the Direct or Indirect Method, always grill with the lid down.

To grill by the Indirect Method on a charcoal grill, arrange hot coals evenly on each side of the charcoal grate. Place food in the center of the cooking grate. A drip pan is useful to collect drippings that can be used for gravies and sauces. It also helps prevent flare-ups when cooking fattier foods.

Rotisserie Cooking

With the rotation of the rotisserie, juices stay in and on the meat, rather than dripping out onto the flames. This self-basting action results in exceptionally succulent meat and deliciously crispy skin. The proper attachment makes it easy to set up your charcoal or gas barbecue grill for rotisserie cooking. Then there's nothing left to do but set the timer. When your roast, chicken, or turkey is done cooking, you'll find the minimal effort of loading the spit has been deliciously rewarded.

advanced techniques, great gadgets

Sometimes the most delicious element of a dish is how it's grilled. Two easy techniques add an extraordinary touch to even the simplest recipes.

Smoke cooking adds authentic flavor and a richer dimension to meats and vegetables. With a few hardwood chunks or chips (and a smoker attachment for gas grills) and a little practice, you can create innovative combinations of meats and woods for a taste customized to your palate.

Rotisserie cooking uses meat's natural juices to your taste buds' advantage. Although no one knows when the first prehistoric cook decided to roast meat slowly and evenly by turning it on a spit over an open flame, we do know the magical effect on flavor and tenderness has been a hit ever since.

Smoke Cooking

To add a touch of smoke flavor to your gas grilling, before preheating the grill, fill the smoker box with wood chips or chunks that have been soaked in water for at least 30 minutes, and fill the water chamber. (For charcoal grilling, simply place soaked chips or chunks directly on the hot coals.) As the grill heats up, the wood will begin to smoke and steam from the water chamber will keep foods moist. Replenish woods and water as needed throughout the grilling time. For best results, start with just a few pieces of wood and experiment to determine the amount that works best for you. (Illustration depicts the smoker box on the Weber® Genesis® Series Gas Barbecue.)

Essentials

An extra-wide **metal spatula** is best for turning burgers, steaks, and delicate fish fillets. Choose one with a long wooden handle and a stainless-steel blade.

A long-handled fork helps lift cooked meats, roasts, and poultry from the grill. Avoid piercing the meat while it's cooking or you may lose tasty juices.

For lightly oiling the cooking grate so that fish and other delicate foods don't stick, choose a long-handled **basting brush** with natural bristles.

Double-prong **skewers** help prevent food from turning while being cooked. Skewers are available in stainless steel, wood, or bamboo. Soak wood and bamboo in water for 30 minutes to prevent burning.

A well-insulated **oven mitt** provides protection from hot tools, pans, utensils, and the grill itself. A gauntlet extension shields the cook's forearm.

A brass-bristle **grill brush** simplifies cleaning. Turn the grill on High to burn off food residue, turn off the grill, and brush off any carbon. Brass is rust-resistant, so it's best for outdoors.

Remember the three T's: **tongs, timer,** and **thermometer.** Long-handled, spring-hinged tongs are great for lifting or turning most foods. A standard kitchen timer reminds you when food needs to be turned, checked, or taken off the grill. An instant-read thermometer ensures that food is cooked thoroughly and tells you when done is about to become overdone.

Essentials

Dijon Wine Sauce

Serve warm with grilled beef, ostrich, or mushrooms.

1½ teaspoons olive oil

4 shallots, finely chopped

½ cup dry white wine

1 cup brown sauce or gravy

1½ tablespoons Dijon mustard

1 teaspoon dried thyme

½ cup crème fraîche

¼ teaspoon salt

⅛ teaspoon ground black pepper

Heat olive oil in small skillet. Add shallots and sauté 2 to 3 minutes. Add white wine and simmer over high heat until reduced to 1 table-spoon liquid. Add brown sauce or gravy, Dijon mustard, and thyme; bring to a simmer. Add crème fraîche; bring to a simmer and remove from heat. Stir in salt and pepper; keep warm.

our favorite sauces

Sauces come in many forms and flavors, from subtle herb sauces to jump-up-and-say-howdy Texas barbecue mops. Some are best added to the dish during the last few minutes of grilling time. Others are slathered on the cooked food after it reaches the table. The best sauces complement rather than complicate the flavors that result from smoke and searing. Here are some of our favorites. But feel free to experiment.

Herb-Butter Sauce

Brush on fish, shellfish, or vegetables after grilling.

½ cup butter

4 teaspoons snipped fresh basil or 1½ teaspoons dried basil

1½ teaspoons snipped fresh oregano or ½ teaspoon dried oregano

1½ teaspoons snipped fresh tarragon or ½ teaspoon dried tarragon

½ teaspoon snipped chives

½ teaspoon snipped fresh thyme or dash dried thyme

Dash pepper

In a saucepan melt butter. Stir in remaining ingredients. Cook 1 to 2 minutes to blend flavors.

Honey-Ginger Peach Sauce

Brush on pork, chicken, or beef in last few minutes of grilling time.

4 medium peaches, peeled and pitted

2 tablespoons honey

2 tablespoons lemon juice

1½ teaspoons minced ginger root

1 teaspoon balsamic vinegar

5 drops hot pepper sauce

Cut 3 of the peaches into large chunks. In a blender or food processor, puree all ingredients until smooth. Pour mixture into a small saucepan. Bring to a boil; reduce heat and simmer uncovered 15 minutes or until slightly thickened, stirring occasionally. Meanwhile, finely chop remaining peach. Stir into sauce. Cover and chill in refrigerator until ready to use.

Hot Pepper Vinegar Sauce

Mop on pork shoulder while it's grilling, then toss more with the pork when you shred it. A little extra on the side is nice, too.

¾ cup apple cider vinegar
¾ cup white vinegar
2 tablespoons sugar
½ teaspoon red pepper flakes
1 teaspoon hot pepper sauce
Salt and pepper to taste

In a medium saucepan combine all ingredients and bring to a boil. Reduce heat and allow to simmer 10 minutes. Serve warm.

Juniper Cream Sauce

A great match with grilled prime rib of beef.

3 tablespoons butter
1 cup sliced fresh mushrooms
3 tablespoons finely chopped shallots
1 quart beef gravy or brown sauce
2 cups dry white wine
15 juniper barries, tied in a cheesecloth sachet

Salt and pepper

½ cup heavy whipping cream
3 tablespoons red currant jelly
2 tablespoons gin

In a medium saucepan melt butter. Add mushrooms and shallots; cook over medium heat 5 minutes or until tender. Add beef gravy, wine, and juniper berry sachet. Simmer over medium heat until liquid is reduced by half. Season with salt and pepper to taste. Meanwhile, in a small mixing bowl, with mixer at medium speed, beat heavy cream until stiff peaks form. Strain reduced sauce; return to saucepan. Stir in red currant jelly and cook over low heat until jelly is dissolved. Stir in gin. Remove from heat. Gently fold in whipped cream. Add salt and pepper to taste.

Paprika Sauce

Excellent with shrimp, lobster, and other seafood.

1 cup butter
3 tablespoons dry white wine
1 tablespoon finely chopped shallots
½ cup heavy cream
½ cup chopped tomato
1 teaspoon Hungarian paprika

In a saucepan melt 1 tablespoon butter. Add wine and shallots; cook rapidly over high heat until liquid is almost evaporated. Add cream, tomatoes, and paprika; cook over medium heat until mixture is reduced and slightly thickened. Add remaining butter; stir until melted. Remove from heat. Serve warm.

Prosperity Sauce (Asian Dipping Sauce)

Serve warm with grilled chicken pieces, particularly wings.

- 3 tablespoons vegetable oil
- 1 teaspoon minced fresh ginger
- 1 scallion, chopped
- ½ cup chicken broth
- 3 tablespoons dark soy sauce
- 2 tablespoons packed brown sugar
- 1 teaspoon chili powder
- ¼ teaspoon crushed red pepper
- 3 teaspoons cornstarch
- 1 tablespoon dry sherry wine

In a small saucepan heat oil. Add ginger and scallions; cook 1 minute or until browned. Add chicken broth, soy sauce, brown sugar, chili powder, and red pepper. Bring to a boil. Dissolve cornstarch in wine; add gradually to liquid, stirring constantly until slightly thickened.

more sauces for grilling

Red Pepper Sauce

Serve with fish or chicken.

- 1 large sweet red pepper, roasted, peeled, and seeded, or ½ cup canned roasted red peppers
- 4 green onions, sliced
- 1 clove garlic, halved
- 2 tablespoons cooking oil
- 2 teaspoons Dijon mustard
- 1 teaspoon honey
- ¾ teaspoon snipped fresh basil or ¼ teaspoon dried basil, crushed
- ⅛ teaspoon salt
- Dash black pepper

Coarsely chop red pepper, set aside. In a skillet cook onions and garlic in oil until tender. Remove from heat; cook slightly. In a blender container or food processor bowl combine red pepper, onion mixture, mustard, honey, basil, salt, and black pepper. Cover; blend or process until smooth. Serve warm.

Weber's Tangy Barbecue Sauce

Perfect for Kansas City-style pork ribs, beef, and chicken.

- ½ cup chopped celery
- 3 tablespoons chopped onion
- 2 tablespoons butter
- 1 cup catsup
- ¼ cup lemon juice
- 2 tablespoons sugar
- 2 tablespons vinegar
- 1 tablespoon Wocestershire sauce
- 1 teaspoon dry mustard
- Dash pepper

In a medium saucepan, cook celery and onion in margarine until tender. Add remaining ingredients and bring to a boil. Reduce heat, cover, and simmer 15 minutes. Serve warm.

Apricot-Ginger Sauce

Add a sweet touch to pork tenderloin or pork roast.

- ½ cup apricot preserves
- 1 tablespoon finely chopped crystallized ginger
- 1 tablespoon sherry vinegar
- ¼ teaspoon dried thyme

In small saucepan, combine all ingredients. Cook over medium heat 2 to 3 minutes until jelly is melted and sauce is hot. Serve warm.

Green Chile Sauce

Add some kick to pork, chicken, or grilled polenta.

- 1 tablespoon roughly chopped roasted green chiles
- 1 medium garlic clove
- 1 tablespoon lime juice
- ½ cup lightly packed fresh cilantro leaves
- ½ teaspoon kosher salt
- ¼ cup sour cream
- ¼ cup mayonnaise

Puree the roasted green chiles, garlic, lime juice, cilantro leaves, and salt in a food processor (or blender). Add the sour cream and mayonnaise and process until the sauce is smooth.

Sweet-and-Sour Sauce

A piquant sauce that pairs especially well with whole fish.

- 3 tablespoons vegetable oil
- 1 large onion, sliced
- ¼ cup minced fresh ginger
- 1 cup sliced sweet gherkins
- 2 cups tomato juice
- 2 tablespoons honey
- 2 tablespoons vinegar
- 1 tablespoon reduced-sodium soy sauce
- 2 tablespoons cornstarch
- Salt and pepper to taste

Heat oil in a large saucepan over high heat. Add onions, ginger, and gherkins and cook for 5 minutes, stirring ocasionally, until tender. Add tomato juice, honey, vinegar, and soy sauce; bring mixture to a boil. Add cornstarch and stir until slightly thickened. Add salt and pepper to taste.

Crisp, Dry Whites

Grilled oysters and clams, many hors d'oeuvres, mildly dressed salads, and grilled vegetables—all love a crisp, dry white with balancing acidity.

Sancerre, Pouilly-Fumé, Muscadet; Chablis below Grand Cru level; Pinot Blanc; Pinot Gris or Pinot Grigio; Orvieto and Verdicchio.

Medium-Bodied Whites

Simply grilled lobster or crab—or even richer fish (tuna, salmon) served without sauces—call for white wines with little or no oak and medium body. They'll complement lighter meats (pork, chicken) too.

Sauvignon Blanc; Gavi; most Alsatians; some Burgundies; unoaked Chardonnay from California, Italy, and southern France.

Rich, Full-Bodied Whites

When cream sauces or soft, rich cheeses are on the menu, pull out the richest white wines you can find.

White Burgundy (St.-Aubin or St.-Romain for value); oaked Chardonnays from California, Australia, and the Pacific Northwest; Sémillon from Australia; Marsanne and Roussanne from California or the Rhône Valley.

Spicy, Aromatic Whites

Often a dish that calls for red wine—such as herb-coated poultry and grilled sausages—will pair wonderfully with a white wine that bursts with fruit and has a floral aroma.

Gewürztraminer; Viognier from California or (as a splurge) Condrieu in France; many Rieslings from Germany and Alsace; semi-sweet Chenin Blanc from the Loire Valley.

pairing wine and grilled food

The same principles that go into matching wine with food cooked in your kitchen will serve you well outdoors—with the added excitement of finding that the character of the meat, fish, or vegetable you've grilled has been intensified by the grilling process itself.

Thinking first of white wines, a mildly flavored meat like pork or turkey, or a delicately flavored fish like trout or halibut will—when simply cooked and served without complicating sauces—pair beautifully with lean white wines. (Think Muscadet from France, a dry Riesling from Germany, or a Pinot Grigio from Italy.) The same holds true for lightly sauced pastas, grilled vegetables, and most shellfish. At the other end of the spectrum, a serving of chicken or veal in a richly seasoned sauce, or an assertive fish like tuna or salmon, requires a wine with similarly bold character: a full-bodied Chardonnay or Sauvignon Blanc from California or Australia, or a fruity, oak-aged Roussanne or Marsanne from the Rhône Valley or California's Central Coast.

Rosé and Blush Wines

The best rosés have balancing acidity, which makes them excellent partners for marinated meats, and sauces incorporating citrus and tomato. They're also peerless aperitifs.

Examples from Italy (Bardolino), France (Tavel, Bandol, Côtes de Provence), Spain, Portugal, and California (Grenache, Pinot Noir, and of course Zinfandel).

Light, Fruity Reds

Perhaps the most flexible of all red wines are these low-alcohol, fruity reds. They pair equally well with roast chicken and hamburger, and many dishes in between.

Beaujolais; Valpolicella; simple Burgundy; Dolcetto, Gamay, Grenache, and Sangiovese; many wines from southern France; unoaked Pinot Noir.

Medium-Bodied Reds

Wines packed with varietal character—often evoking the colorful regions of their origin—are hard to top when foods of equivalent depth of flavor are on the menu.

Cru Beaujolais (Moulin-a-Vent, Brouilly); most Bordeaux; Burgundy Côtes and Villages; Chianti; Côtes du Rhône-Villages; Crozes-Hermitage and Gigondas; Rioja; Shiraz blends.

Full-Bodied Reds

The heartiest, most savory dishes—those built on a firm foundation of beef, lamb, mushrooms, or full-flavored cheeses—come into their own when wines of powerful depth and intensity are served alongside.

Barolo and Barbaresco; oaked Cabernet Sauvignon; high-end Rhônes (Châteauneuf-du-Pape, Cornas, Côte Rôtie); Australian Shiraz; old-vine Zinfandel.

The other important factor to bear in mind is a dish's body—whether it will strike your palate as lean or rich. (For "rich" some people like to use the term "fatty," but it's misleading—richness comes from many other flavor components besides fat.) A dish that offers a lean "mouthfeel" (veal, shellfish, simply grilled meats) will pair well with wines that are on the lighter and simpler side. Meanwhile, a rich-tasting dish—a grilled filet mignon with a red-wine sauce, say—calls for a wine that is intensely flavored and of medium to full body.

These general rules will get you started, and you may find you never need to go beyond them. If you do decide to pursue the fascinating realm of food-and-wine matching in greater depth, you'll find an endless variety of combinations to explore . . . options limited only by the number of foods you can find to grill, seasonings you can contrive to add, and wines you can track down to taste and enjoy.

menu planner

The recipes in this book have been developed to offer you a full array of possibilities for entertaining. Follow any of the suggested menus here or use them as starting points from which to create your own. When planning any grilled menu, think first about whether you and your guests are in the mood for something simple or sophisticated. Then decide if you'd like to serve three separate courses or maybe just one or two? If you plan on one or two courses with grilled side dishes, look for recipes that you can prepare ahead or cook during the same time as the main course. Also keep a sense of balance in mind and try to offer a wide variety of ingredients throughout the meal. For example, if the main course involves a particularly rich or heavy meat recipe, serve a lighter dish built on seafood or vegetables before it. There's no great secret to menu planning; above all, grill what you like and have fun doing it.

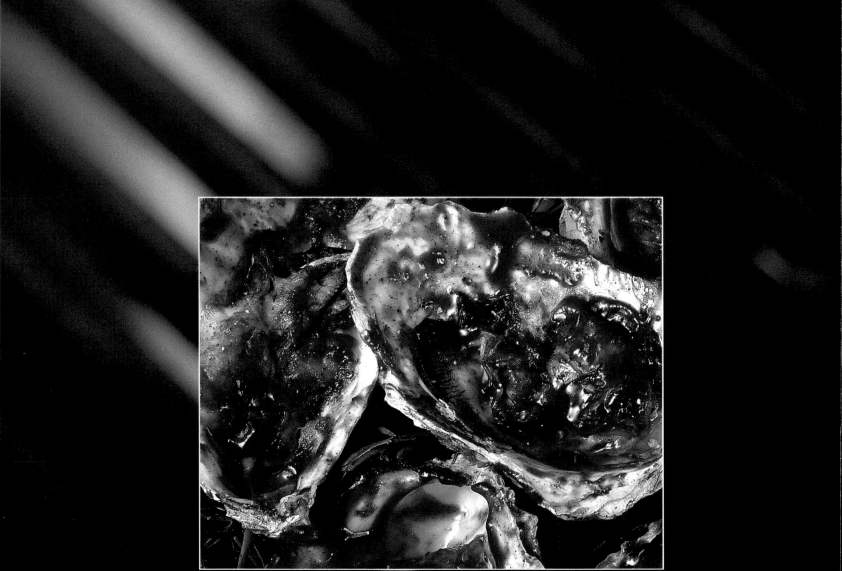

starters

Have you noticed that from the moment the grill gets hot, people expect to see great things happen? To fulfill their anticipation, it's wise to serve a captivating starter or two until the main course is ready. Those of us who appreciate any excuse to eat with our hands like to see finger food as an option. Grilled pita bread and the Middle Eastern dip baba ghanoush, for example, always get rave reviews—especially if the dip is made in the traditional way, with eggplants grilled over flames. For deceptively simple but elegant recipes, consider barbecued oysters or grilled bliss potatoes topped with sour cream and caviar.

Kabobs have been with us almost as long as there have been food, fire, and wooden sticks, and people still love them. You can prepare a winning version of beef and chicken satay with peanut sauce or prosciutto-wrapped shrimp in a matter of minutes. Of course, certain events call for something a bit more substantial to serve as a first course, so we also offer grilled butternut squash soup or smoked corn chowder.

So grab your drink and a pair of tongs. Once you get started, you won't want to leave the grill. And, with the following recipes in your repertoire, no one else will want you to leave, either.

Prosciutto-Wrapped Shrimp

Prosciutto is an Italian-style ham that has been seasoned, usually salt-cured, and air-dried rather than smoked. Often sold in paper-thin slices, it wraps easily around large shrimp and benefits from quick cooking. For a showy presentation, prop up these always popular hors d'oeuvres in a glass filled with colored marbles.

DIRECT/MEDIUM HEAT

16 **jumbo shrimp (about 1 pound), peeled and deveined**

1 **tablespoon finely chopped garlic**

1½ **tablespoons finely chopped fresh dill**

¼ **teaspoon freshly ground pepper**

8 **paper-thin slices prosciutto (about 4 ounces)**

Olive oil for brushing shrimp

Metal skewers (or bamboo skewers, soaked in water for at least 30 minutes)

IN A MEDIUM BOWL, combine the shrimp, garlic, dill, and pepper. Toss the shrimp to coat them lightly. Cut the prosciutto slices in half lengthwise. Wrap each shrimp in a half slice of prosciutto, then thread it onto the end of a skewer. Lightly brush the shrimp with olive oil.

Grill the shrimp directly over medium heat, turning once, until just opaque, about 4 minutes total. Serve warm or at room temperature.

MAKES 16 SKEWERS

Caponata Bruschetta

Caponata—a Sicilian mixture of eggplant, onion, tomato, olives, capers, and often anchovies—can be served as a salad, a side dish, or a relish. Mounded on toasted Italian bread with goat cheese, it makes a delicious hors d'oeuvre or appetizer and is a good way to use up day-old bread.

DIRECT/MEDIUM HEAT

FOR THE CAPONATA:

- 1 **medium eggplant, about 12 ounces, cut crosswise into ½-inch-thick slices**
- **Kosher salt**
- 1 **small yellow onion, cut crosswise into ½-inch-thick slices**
- ⅓ **cup olive oil**
- 1 **medium tomato, seeded and roughly chopped**
- 15 **kalamata olives, pitted and finely chopped**
- 2 **tablespoons finely chopped fresh basil**
- 1 **tablespoon capers, drained**
- 2 **teaspoons balsamic vinegar**
- 1 **teaspoon finely chopped garlic**
- **Freshly ground pepper**

- 8 **slices Italian or other coarse country bread, about ½ inch thick and 4 inches wide**
- 4 **ounces fresh goat cheese, crumbled**

TO MAKE THE CAPONATA: Rub both sides of the eggplant slices thoroughly with salt. Allow them to sit in a colander placed in the sink or over a plate for about 30 minutes to draw out their bitter juices. Rinse the eggplant well and pat dry. Brush both sides of the eggplant and onion slices with the olive oil.

Grill the eggplant and onion slices directly over medium heat, turning once, until tender, 10 to 12 minutes total. Allow to cool. Coarsely chop the eggplant and onion slices and transfer to a medium bowl. Add the tomato, olives, basil, capers, vinegar, and garlic and mix well. Season with salt and pepper to taste.

Grill the bread slices directly over medium heat, turning once, until toasted, 2 to 3 minutes total. Divide the goat cheese evenly among the bread slices, spreading it with a knife. Spoon the caponata over the goat cheese, again dividing evenly. Serve at room temperature.

MAKES 8 PIECES

Thin-Crusted Pizza with Chicken, Kalamata Olives, and Fontina Cheese

You may never cook a pizza in your oven again after you've tasted one off the grill. The delicate crust comes out crisp and singed in spots, but still chewy in the center, and it picks up the wonderful smoky flavors of the grill. The toppings included here should be looked upon as suggestions only. Substitute whatever you prefer.

DIRECT/MEDIUM HEAT

FOR THE DOUGH:

1 envelope active dry yeast

½ teaspoon sugar

⅔ cup warm water (105°F to 115°F)

2 to 3 cups all-purpose flour

1 teaspoon kosher salt

1 teaspoon freshly ground pepper

2 tablespoons olive oil, plus olive oil for brushing crusts

FOR THE TOPPING:

3 cups thinly sliced grilled chicken meat

¾ cup sliced, pitted kalamata olives

4 cups shredded fontina cheese

1 cup thinly sliced red onion

2 tablespoons finely chopped fresh parsley

TO MAKE THE DOUGH: In a medium bowl, combine the yeast, sugar, and water. Stir briefly and let stand until foamy, 5 to 10 minutes. Add 2 cups of the flour, the salt, pepper, and the 2 tablespoons olive oil. Stir with your fingers until the dough holds together. Transfer the dough to a lightly floured work surface and knead until smooth, 8 to 10 minutes. Shape into a ball and place in a lightly oiled bowl. Turn the ball to cover the surface with oil. Cover the bowl with plastic wrap and set aside in a warm place until the dough doubles in size, 1 to 1½ hours.

Punch down the dough in the bowl. Transfer it to a lightly floured work surface and cut into 4 equal pieces. Roll out each piece into an 8-inch round about ⅛ inch thick. Lightly brush both sides of each round with olive oil and place the rounds on baking sheets.

Gently slide the crusts from the baking sheet onto the grill and cook, uncovered, directly over medium heat until grill marks are clearly visible, about 2 minutes. Don't worry if the crusts bubble; they will deflate when you turn them over. Transfer the crusts to the baking sheets, with the grilled sides facing up.

Distribute the chicken, olives, cheese, onion, and parsley evenly among the crusts. Transfer the pizzas again from the baking sheet to the grill and cook, covered, directly over medium heat until the crusts are crisp and the cheese is melted, 3 to 4 more minutes.

Serve the pizzas warm, cut into wedges.

MAKES 4 EIGHT-INCH PIZZAS

Teriyaki Chicken Wings

Most chicken wing partisans are less interested in the little bit of meat on the bones than they are in the high proportion of skin, which crackles and crisps over the fire. Picking up these appetizers in your fingers and gnawing on them with no regard for table manners gets a playful picnic off to the right start. The Japanese marinade—a blend of soy sauce, sugar, ginger, and other seasonings—also tastes great on shrimp and flank steak.

DIRECT/MEDIUM HEAT

½ **cup soy sauce**

¼ **cup lightly packed brown sugar**

1 **tablespoon finely chopped garlic**

1 **tablespoon grated fresh ginger**

½ **teaspoon cayenne pepper**

1 **tablespoon Asian sesame oil**

20 **chicken wings (3½ to 4 pounds)**

2 **tablespoons sesame seeds**

IN A SMALL SAUCEPAN, combine the soy sauce, brown sugar, garlic, ginger, cayenne pepper, and ¼ cup water. Bring to a boil, stirring to dissolve the brown sugar. Allow to cool to room temperature. Add the sesame oil and stir well.

With a sharp knife, remove the tips from the chicken wings. Put the chicken wings in a large lock-top bag and add the soy sauce mixture. Seal and marinate in the refrigerator for at least 1 hour or as long as 4 hours. Turn the bag occasionally to coat all of the wings.

Remove the wings from the bag. Sprinkle evenly with the sesame seeds. Pour the marinade into a small saucepan over high heat, bring to a boil for one minute, and remove from the heat.

Grill the chicken wings directly over medium heat, turning once and basting occasionally with the boiled marinade, until the juices run clear, 14 to 16 minutes total.

Serve warm or at room temperature.

MAKES 20 CHICKEN WINGS

Beef and Chicken Satay with Peanut Dipping Sauce

Rich in the flavors of Southeast Asia, satay lends itself to many variations, including chicken, beef, pork, and seafood. Keep in mind that whatever you thread onto the skewers must be small and tender enough to cook quickly. When using flank steak, cut it on the bias and against the grain to ensure that it will be tender when grilled.

DIRECT/MEDIUM HEAT

FOR THE BEEF AND CHICKEN:

- 1 **shallot, roughly chopped**
- 2 **garlic cloves, roughly chopped**
- ½-**inch piece fresh ginger, peeled and roughly chopped**
- 2 **teaspoons hot chile sauce**
- 1 **teaspoon ground cumin**
- ½ **teaspoon ground coriander**
- ½ **teaspoon kosher salt**
- 2 **tablespoons peanut oil**
- 8 **ounces flank steak**
- 8 **ounces boneless, skinless chicken breast**

FOR THE PEANUT SAUCE:

- ¾ **cup dry-roasted peanuts**
- ¾ **cup coconut milk**
- 1 **tablespoon brown sugar**
- 1 **tablespoon fresh lime juice**
- ¼ **teaspoon red curry paste**
- 1 **tablespoon finely chopped fresh cilantro**

Metal skewers (or bamboo skewers, soaked in water for at least 30 minutes)

IN A FOOD PROCESSOR OR BLENDER, combine the shallot, garlic, ginger, chile sauce, cumin, coriander, salt, and ¼ cup water. Puree to create a paste. In a small sauté pan over medium-high heat, fry the paste in the 2 tablespoons peanut oil until it boils and the aroma is apparent, 1 to 2 minutes. Allow to cool to room temperature.

Cut the flank steak on the bias and against the grain into slices ⅓ inch thick and 5 to 6 inches long. Cut the chicken into slices ½ inch thick and 5 to 6 inches long. Place the beef and chicken slices in a medium bowl and toss with the paste to coat thoroughly. Cover with plastic wrap and marinate in the refrigerator for at least 30 minutes or as long as 4 hours. Thread the beef and chicken slices on the skewers.

To make the peanut sauce: In a food processor, grind the peanuts until they are as fine as cornmeal. In a medium saucepan, combine the ground peanuts with ½ cup of the coconut milk, the brown sugar, lime juice, red curry paste, and ½ cup water. Bring to a boil, then reduce the heat to a simmer and cook, stirring occasionally, until the sauce is as thick as yogurt, 10 to 15 minutes. Stir in the cilantro. Keep warm over low heat. If the sauce thickens too much, stir in as much of the remaining coconut milk as needed to achieve a good consistency.

Brush the cooking grate with peanut oil. Grill the beef directly over medium heat, turning once, for about 4 minutes for medium-rare. Grill the chicken directly over medium heat, turning once, until opaque throughout, about 4 minutes.

Serve the satay warm with the peanut sauce.

MAKES 10 TO 15 SKEWERS

Bliss Potatoes with Sour Cream and Caviar

A party takes on an elegant tone when it opens with caviar. A trace of smokiness on the small red potatoes is a seductive foil for the tiny black pearls from the Caspian Sea. To complete the scene, serve a dry sparkling wine or vodka martini.

DIRECT/MEDIUM HEAT

- 8 red new potatoes, each about 1½ inches in diameter
- ¼ cup olive oil
  Kosher salt
- ⅓ cup sour cream
- 2 ounces sevruga or osetra caviar
- 16 fresh chervil leaves

PUT THE POTATOES IN A MEDIUM SAUCEPAN half-filled with salted water. Bring to a boil over high heat, reduce the heat to a simmer, and cook until the potatoes are tender, 15 to 20 minutes. Drain and cool until easy to handle.

Cut a thin slice off the ends of each potato, then cut the potatoes in half vertically. With a melon baller, remove a small scoop of flesh from each half. Put the potatoes in a medium bowl. Drizzle with the olive oil and season with salt to taste. Toss to coat thoroughly.

Grill the potato halves directly over medium heat, turning once, until the skins wrinkle and the halves are tender but not mushy, 8 to 10 minutes total. Remove from the grill and allow to cool slightly.

Spoon 1 teaspoon of the sour cream into the hollow in each potato half. Top with the caviar, dividing evenly. Garnish with the chervil leaves. Serve at room temperature.

MAKES 4 SERVINGS

Baba Ghanoush

This traditional Middle Eastern dip can tame fierce appetites before a barbecue. Don't be afraid you will overcook the eggplant; it should grill until the skin begins to blister and the smoky center is completely soft. If you prefer a very smooth dip, stir in a few tablespoons of plain yogurt.

DIRECT/HIGH HEAT

- 2 **globe eggplants, about 1 pound each**
- 1 **large garlic clove**
- 3 **tablespoons tahini (sesame seed paste)**
- 2 **tablespoons fresh lemon juice**
- ¼ **teaspoon ground cumin**
- ¼ **teaspoon paprika**
- ½ **teaspoon kosher salt**
  Freshly ground pepper
- 3 **tablespoons plain yogurt (optional)**
- 8 **pita bread pockets**

GRILL THE EGGPLANTS directly over high heat, turning occasionally, until the skins are blistered and the flesh is easily pierced with a fork, 15 to 20 minutes. Remove from the grill and allow to cool. Cut the eggplants in half lengthwise and scoop out the flesh.

In a food processor or blender, combine the eggplant flesh, garlic, tahini, lemon juice, cumin, paprika, and salt. Puree until smooth. Season with pepper to taste. Add the yogurt if a very smooth dip is desired.

Grill the pita bread directly over high heat, turning once, until toasted, 1 to 2 minutes. (For easier dipping, cut the pitas into wedges before grilling.) Serve warm or at room temperature with the dip.

MAKES 1½ TO 2 CUPS

Swordfish Kabobs with Roasted Red Pepper Aioli

Paprika is the primary seasoning in these fish kabobs, and its flavor can run from mild and slightly sweet to somewhat hot and bitter. Hungarian paprika generally offers the highest quality and is preferable for this dish.

DIRECT/MEDIUM HEAT

FOR THE AIOLI:

2 red bell peppers

2 teaspoons chopped garlic

3 tablespoons fresh lemon juice

½ cup mayonnaise

¼ teaspoon kosher salt

   Pinch cayenne pepper

3 tablespoons olive oil

2 tablespoons fresh lemon juice

1 tablespoon paprika, preferably Hungarian

1 teaspoon chili powder

1 teaspoon kosher salt

2 pounds skinless swordfish fillets, cut into 1½-inch cubes

Metal skewers (or bamboo skewers soaked in water for at least 30 minutes)

TO MAKE THE AIOLI: Grill the bell peppers directly over medium heat, turning occasionally, until the skin is completely black and blistered, 10 to 12 minutes. Transfer the peppers to a paper bag, seal it tightly, and let the peppers cool for 15 minutes, during which time the skins will loosen. Remove and discard the skins, stems, and seeds. In a food processor or blender, combine the roasted peppers, garlic, and lemon juice and puree until smooth. In a small bowl, combine the purée with the mayonnaise, salt, and cayenne pepper. Mix well, cover, and refrigerate until ready to use. Bring to room temperature before serving.

In a medium bowl, stir together the olive oil, lemon juice, paprika, chili powder, and salt. Add the swordfish and toss to coat thoroughly. Cover and marinate in the refrigerator for about 30 minutes.

Thread the swordfish onto skewers. Grill directly over medium heat, turning occasionally, until just opaque, 5 to 6 minutes total. Serve warm with the aioli.

MAKES 4 TO 6 SERVINGS

Barbecued Oysters, West Coast Style

Exuberant Californians, who are known to put almost anything on the grill, have made barbecued oysters a heated issue. Some of them say that oysters should be grilled unshucked, so they steam their shells open. Others will tell you that shucking them first, then grilling them in a buttery barbecue sauce, is the best approach. One definite advantage of the latter method is that once the oysters are cooked, there's nothing left to do but slurp them down.

DIRECT/HIGH HEAT

FOR THE SAUCE:

- 1 tablespoon unsalted butter
- 1 teaspoon minced garlic
- 2 tablespoons freshly squeezed lemon juice
- 2 tablespoons mild chili sauce

- 12 fresh oysters

TO MAKE THE BARBECUE SAUCE: In a small sauté pan over medium heat, cook the butter and garlic, stirring occasionally, until the garlic aroma is apparent and the butter begins to brown, 2 to 3 minutes. Remove from the heat and add the lemon juice and chili sauce. Mix until well blended.

To open the oysters: Grip each oyster flat side up in a folded kitchen towel. Find a small opening between the shells near the hinge and pry open with an oyster knife. Try to keep the juices in the shell. Loosen the oyster from the shell by running the oyster knife carefully underneath the body. Discard the top, flatter shell, keeping the oyster in the bottom, deeper shell.

Spoon ½ teaspoon of barbecue sauce over each oyster. Grill the oysters directly over high heat, When the sauce boils inside the shell, after 2 to 3 minutes, cook oysters for 1 to 2 minutes more. Serve warm.

MAKES 12 OYSTERS

Smoked Corn Chowder

This soulful soup gets its heft from chunks of tender potato and by pureeing some of the corn. To extract the maximum flavor from the corn, scrape the cobs with the back of a knife to release their milky liquid for use in the purée, then simmer the cobs in the soup right up until the time you are ready to serve.

INDIRECT/LOW HEAT

- 4 **ears of corn, husks and silks removed**
- 3 **slices bacon, cut into ½-inch dice**
- 1 **small yellow onion, cut into ½-inch dice**
- 2 **red bell peppers, cut into ½-inch dice**
- ¼ **cup all-purpose flour**
- 5 **cups chicken stock**
- 2 **large russet potatoes, peeled and cut into ½-inch dice**
- 1 **bay leaf**
- ½ **cup half-and-half**
- ½ **teaspoon Worcestershire sauce**
- ¼ **teaspoon Tabasco sauce**
- 2 **tablespoons finely chopped fresh parsley**
- **Kosher salt**
- **Freshly ground pepper**

- **Mesquite or hickory chips, soaked in water for 30 minutes**

FOLLOW THE GRILL'S INSTRUCTIONS for using wood chips. Grill the corn indirectly over low heat, turning occasionally, until lightly browned, 20 to 25 minutes. Remove the corn and allow to cool. With a sharp knife, cut the kernels from the cobs and set aside. With the back of the knife, scrape the cobs to release the milky liquid into a small bowl. Set aside the cobs. In a food processor or blender, puree half of the kernels with all of the milky liquid. Set aside the whole and pureed kernels.

Place a large saucepan or Dutch oven on the stovetop or side burner over medium heat. Cook the bacon, stirring occasionally, until crispy, about 10 minutes. Raise the heat to medium-high. Add the onion and cook, stirring occasionally, until translucent, about 4 minutes. Add the red bell peppers and cook, stirring occasionally, until the peppers are tender, about 6 minutes. Sprinkle the flour over the vegetables. Cook for about 1 minute, stirring occasionally. Raise the heat to high. Gradually add the chicken stock, whisking to prevent the flour from forming lumps. Bring to a boil, then lower the heat to a simmer, whisking constantly. Add the whole and pureed corn kernels along with the cobs (cut in half if necessary), potatoes, and bay leaf. Cook, uncovered, until the potatoes are tender, about 20 minutes, stirring occasionally to prevent the corn from scorching on the bottom of the pan. Remove and discard the cobs and the bay leaf. Add the half-and-half, Worcestershire sauce, Tabasco sauce, and parsley. Season with salt and pepper to taste. Return to a simmer for 1 minute.

Ladle into warmed bowls and serve immediately.

MAKES 6 SERVINGS

Grilled Butternut Squash and Ginger Soup with Spiced Peanuts

Winter squashes such as butternut and acorn have an earthy sweetness that the grill accentuates. The spiced peanuts that give crunch to this soup can be prepared ahead of time and stored in an airtight container at room temperature. You'll need willpower, however, to resist munching on them.

INDIRECT/MEDIUM HEAT

FOR THE SPICED PEANUTS:

1½ cups roasted peanuts
    (not dry-roasted)

2 tablespoons peanut oil

1½ teaspoons ground ginger

1 tablespoon finely chopped garlic

2 teaspoons finely chopped
    fresh cilantro

½ teaspoon Chinese five-spice powder

¼ teaspoon cayenne pepper

FOR THE SOUP:

1 large butternut squash,
    about 3½ pounds

    Olive oil for brushing squash

1 large leek

2 tablespoons unsalted butter

4 teaspoons grated fresh ginger

5 to 6 cups chicken stock

    Kosher salt

    Freshly ground pepper

TO MAKE THE SPICED PEANUTS: In a small bowl, combine the peanuts, peanut oil, ground ginger, garlic, cilantro, five-spice powder, and cayenne. Toss well to coat the peanuts evenly, then transfer them to a sheet of aluminum foil large enough to hold them. Pull the corners of the foil together and close the pouch. Place the pouch over indirect medium heat for about 5 minutes. Carefully remove the pouch and allow to cool.

To make the soup: With a large, heavy knife, cut the squash in half through the stem and discard the seeds. Brush the cut sides of the squash with olive oil. Grill, cut side down, indirectly over medium heat until the skin can be easily pierced with the tip of a sharp knife, about 1 hour. (The squash will not be completely cooked at this point.) Remove the squash from the grill and allow to cool. With a large spoon, scoop the flesh from the squash and discard the skin.

Cut off most of the tough green top from the leek. Cut the leek in half lengthwise. Wash under cold running water to remove any dirt trapped between the layers. Cut crosswise into ½-inch pieces.

In a large saucepan over medium-high heat, melt the butter. Add the leek and ginger and cook, stirring occasionally, until the leeks are tender, about 5 minutes. Add 5 cups of the chicken stock. Bring to a boil and carefully add the squash. Reduce the heat to very low and cook, stirring occasionally, about 20 minutes. Puree the soup, in batches, in a food processor or blender. Return the soup to the saucepan. If it seems too thick, add as much of the remaining 1 cup stock as needed to achieve a good consistency. Season with salt and pepper to taste.

Serve warm, garnished with the spiced peanuts.

MAKES 6 SERVINGS

America's unabashed enthusiasm for grilled meats has returned with vigor, and it now extends far beyond hot dogs and hamburgers. Magnificent cuts of beef, pork, lamb, and veal—not to mention venison and buffalo—are regularly appearing at backyard barbecues.

Some of us prefer the naturally tender cuts that come from protected and seldom exercised parts of the animal, such as the tenderloin, rib section, and loin (which sits beneath the ribs).

meats

These cuts cook to a succulent texture relatively quickly. Try our recipe for filet mignon or lamb chops and you'll understand completely.

Other people identify more with authentic barbecue, which relies on tougher, coarser-grained cuts from well-exercised muscles such as the neck, shoulders, and legs. These cuts need to cook longer to break down sinews and connective tissues, but the payoff comes in the form of unparalleled flavor. For proof, see how low, slow heat can transform a tough pork shoulder into soft shreds of delectable meat in our authentic pulled pork sandwich.

You'll find that an instant-read thermometer is invaluable for grilling any meats thicker than one inch, because it allows you to use the temperature guidelines given within the recipes and on page 204. And for superior taste, always look for the highest grade of meat possible—preferably prime or choice.

Coffee-and-Pepper-Crusted New York Steaks

In this unusual recipe, the piquancy of peppercorns meets the mellowness of coffee beans with stellar results. Turn the steaks when you see beads of juice on the surface. When the steaks are cooked to your preference, allow them to rest for a few minutes before serving so the juices that have been forced to the edges can ease back into the center.

DIRECT/HIGH HEAT

- **2 tablespoons whole coffee beans**
- **2 tablespoons whole black peppercorns**
- **4 New York (strip) steaks, each about ¾ pound and 1 inch thick**
- **Vegetable oil for brushing cooking grate**
- **Kosher salt**

COARSELY GRIND THE COFFEE BEANS and peppercorns in a food processor or coffee grinder. Press the mixture evenly on both sides of the steaks.

Lightly brush the cooking grate with vegetable oil. Grill the steaks directly over high heat, turning once, for about 8 to 10 minutes, or until cooked to desired doneness.

Remove the steaks from the grill. Season both sides with salt. Allow to rest for 2 to 3 minutes before serving. Serve warm.

MAKES 4 SERVINGS

WINE NOTES: *Try a rich, mellow red with lots of fruit and very little tannin: a young California Merlot or Zinfandel, or a fully mature Cabernet Sauvignon from a top vintage.*

Bodacious Porterhouse Steaks
with Sexy Barbecue Sauce

Once you have masterfully grilled an outrageously thick porterhouse steak, cut it into slices that drip with precious juices, and served it with a barbecue sauce so seductive that it has to be called sexy, you have experienced a grilling rite of passage. To make the most of the irresistibly marbled sirloin strip on one side of the bone, and the supple meat of the tenderloin on the other side, cook these porterhouses over direct heat with a watchful eye.

DIRECT/HIGH HEAT

FOR THE SAUCE:

½ cup dry red wine

½ cup ketchup

¼ cup dark molasses

1 tablespoon Dijon mustard

1 tablespoon Worcestershire sauce

2 tablespoons red wine vinegar

½ teaspoon chili powder

½ teaspoon kosher salt

½ teaspoon celery seeds

¼ teaspoon curry powder

¼ teaspoon ground cumin

2 porterhouse steaks, each about 2 pounds and 1½ inches thick

Vegetable oil for brushing steaks

Kosher salt

Freshly ground black pepper

TO MAKE THE SAUCE: In a medium saucepan, combine the wine, ketchup, molasses, mustard, Worcestershire sauce, vinegar, chili powder, salt, celery seeds, curry powder, cumin, and ½ cup water. Mix well. Bring to a simmer over medium heat and cook uncovered, stirring occasionally, until about ⅔ cup remains, about 30 minutes. Allow to cool to room temperature.

Lightly brush both sides of the steaks with vegetable oil and season generously with salt and pepper. Grill the first side of the steaks directly over high heat for 6 minutes. Turn the steaks over and cook the second side for 5 minutes. Continue to cook the steaks to desired doneness.

Remove the steaks from the grill. Season again with salt and pepper. Let rest for 3 to 5 minutes, during which time the internal temperature will rise about 5 degrees. You can serve the steaks whole, or cut the sirloin strips and tenderloins away from the bones, then cut the meat into ¼-inch-thick slices. Serve warm with the barbecue sauce.

MAKES 4 SERVINGS

WINE NOTES: *Choose a hearty red to match these hearty flavors: a ripe California Zinfandel, Petite Sirah, or rustic Carignane. Otherwise, try a full-flavored, somewhat malty beer—a Bock or "old brown" lager, for example.*

Filet Mignon with Shoestring Potatoes

For the kind of tenderness that can be cut with a butter knife, filet mignon has no equal among steaks. Dressed in a lusty wine sauce and accompanied with shoestring potatoes, it speaks directly to those who appreciate classic bistro fare.

DIRECT/MEDIUM HEAT

FOR THE SAUCE:

- 2 tablespoons olive oil
- 1 medium carrot, roughly chopped
- 2 celery stalks, roughly chopped
- 1 medium yellow onion, roughly chopped
- 5 medium garlic cloves, roughly chopped
- 2 tablespoons tomato paste
- 3 cups beef broth
- 2 cups dry red wine
- ½ cup balsamic vinegar
- 3 bay leaves
- 2 tablespoons fresh rosemary leaves
- 1½ teaspoons whole black peppercorns
- Salt and freshly ground black pepper

FOR THE POTATOES:

- 6 cups peanut oil
- 2 large baking potatoes, peeled and placed in a bowl of water to prevent discoloration
- Kosher salt

- 4 filets mignons, each about 8 ounces and 1½ inches thick
- Vegetable oil for brushing steaks
- Salt and freshly ground black pepper

TO MAKE THE SAUCE: In a large saucepan over high heat, warm the olive oil. Add the carrot, celery, and onion, and cook, stirring occasionally, until the vegetables are browned, 6 to 8 minutes. Add the garlic and cook, stirring occasionally, for about 2 more minutes. Reduce the heat to medium, add the tomato paste, and cook, stirring often, for about 2 more minutes. Add the broth, wine, vinegar, bay leaves, rosemary, and peppercorns. Simmer, uncovered, for 45 minutes. Strain through a sieve into a medium saucepan, pressing down on the solids with the back of a spoon. Continue to simmer until about ½ cup liquid remains, about 45 more minutes. Season with salt and pepper to taste. Remove from the heat.

To make the shoestring potatoes: In an electric fryer, heat the peanut oil to 350°F. Meanwhile, using a mandoline or sharp knife, cut the potatoes lengthwise into strips ¼ inch wide and ⅟₁₆ inch thick. Immediately return the potatoes to the water. When both potatoes have been cut, drain and replace the water until it is no longer cloudy. Dry the potatoes in batches in a salad spinner. Carefully add the potatoes in small batches to the hot oil. Cook, stirring gently with metal tongs, until crisp and golden brown, about 5 minutes. Remove with a slotted spoon, and place on a baking sheet lined with paper towels. Immediately sprinkle with salt, and keep warm.

Brush both sides of the steaks with vegetable oil and season with salt and pepper. Grill directly over medium heat, turning once, until cooked to desired doneness. The steaks will take 11 to 13 minutes total to reach medium-rare. Remove the steaks from the grill and allow to rest for 2 to 3 minutes, during which time the internal temperature will rise about 5 degrees. Warm the sauce over low heat and serve with the steaks and the shoestring potatoes.

MAKES 4 SERVINGS

WINE NOTES: *The king of red wines for the king of steaks: a classic Cabernet Sauvignon from California. Choose an older wine, one that's not too tannic but still retains a core of lip-smacking fruit.*

Mediterranean Flank Steak Sandwich in Pita Bread

An inexpensive cut of meat from the belly, flank steak has a broad surface area that picks up a great deal of flavor as it sizzles on the cooking grate. If you slice flank steak thinly against the grain, you cut many of its fibers, making it tender enough for sandwiches.

DIRECT/MEDIUM HEAT

FOR THE SAUCE:

1 cup plain yogurt, nonfat if desired

½ cup peeled, seeded, and finely diced cucumber

2 tablespoons finely chopped fresh basil

½ teaspoon garlic salt

⅛ teaspoon cayenne pepper

FOR THE STEAK:

2 large red onions, cut crosswise into ½-inch-thick slices

3 tablespoons olive oil

2 teaspoons garlic salt

2 teaspoons dried oregano

¼ teaspoon freshly ground pepper

1 beef flank steak, about 1½ pounds

4 pita bread pockets

4 plum tomatoes, cut crosswise into ¼-inch-thick slices

4 large leaves lettuce

TO MAKE THE SAUCE: In a small bowl, mix together the yogurt, cucumber, basil, garlic salt, and cayenne pepper. Cover and refrigerate until ready to use. Bring to room temperature before serving.

Lightly brush both sides of the onion slices with about 1½ tablespoons of the olive oil. Grill them directly over medium heat, turning once, until tender, 12 to 14 minutes total.

In a small bowl, combine the garlic salt, oregano, and pepper with the remaining 1½ tablespoons olive oil. Spread this mixture evenly over both sides of the flank steak. Grill the flank steak directly over medium heat, turning once, until cooked to desired doneness, 10 to 11 minutes for rare or 12 to 14 minutes for medium-rare. Grilling the steak longer will dry out the meat.

Remove the flank steak from the grill and allow it to rest for 2 to 3 minutes. Then thinly slice it on the diagonal across the grain. Fill each pita bread pocket with steak, onions, tomatoes, and lettuce. Drizzle some sauce inside. Serve warm or at room temperature.

MAKES 4 SERVINGS

WINE NOTES: *Choose a fruity red wine low in both alcohol and tannins (such as a Beaujolais-Villages), or else a beer with enough bite to cut through the yogurt: an assertive pale ale from Britain or the Pacific Northwest.*

Steak and Tomato Kabobs
with Avocado Cream

If you like guacamole, you'll recognize some of its addictive flavors in this recipe. Most of the heat and spice come from the well-seasoned meat, while the avocado cream plays a cool and creamy supporting role. The tomatoes cook just long enough to break down and release their juices.

DIRECT/MEDIUM HEAT

FOR THE RUB:

1 teaspoon minced garlic

1 teaspoon dry mustard

2 teaspoons kosher salt

1 teaspoon chili powder

½ teaspoon paprika

½ teaspoon ground coriander

½ teaspoon ground cumin

FOR THE SAUCE:

1 Haas avocado

2-inch piece seedless cucumber

¼ cup sour cream

¼ cup thinly sliced scallions

¼ cup chopped fresh dill

3 or 4 dashes Tabasco sauce

Juice of 1 lime

Kosher salt

2 pounds top sirloin

18 to 24 cherry tomatoes

Vegetable oil for brushing cooking grate

8 metal skewers (or wooden skewers soaked in water for 30 minutes)

TO MAKE THE DRY RUB: In a medium bowl, mix together the garlic, mustard, salt, chili powder, paprika, coriander, and cumin.

To make the sauce: Pit and peel the avocado and place in a food processor or blender. Peel the cucumber and cut into 1-inch dice. Add to the processor or blender with the sour cream, scallions, dill, Tabasco, lime juice, and ¼ cup water. Puree until smooth. Season with salt to taste. Pour the sauce into a small bowl, cover, and refrigerate until ready to use. (This may be made up to 1 day ahead.) Bring to room temperature before serving.

Cut the beef into 1½-inch pieces. Place them in a medium bowl and coat with the dry rub. Thread 3 tomatoes and 3 or 4 pieces of beef onto each skewer, separating the pieces of beef with tomatoes.

Brush the cooking grate with vegetable oil. Grill the kabobs directly over medium heat, turning once, for 7 to 8 minutes total. The skin of the tomatoes should be lightly charred and starting to slip off. Serve warm with the avocado sauce.

MAKES 6 TO 8 SKEWERS

WINE NOTES: *Avocado and tomato spell summer to most people. Beers have seasons, too: Try a Belgian saison with these kabobs, or (easier to find) a British or American summer ale.*

Prime Rib with Texas Dry Rub

In Texas, where meat means beef and dry rubs range from hot to fiery to downright dangerous, cooks know how to handle prime rib. Their most reliably delicious way is to coat the meat with toasted spices and then grill it over indirect heat. No turning. No basting. No flare-ups. Cowboys have been known to cry over food this good.

INDIRECT/MEDIUM HEAT

FOR THE RUB:

2 tablespoons cumin seeds

2 tablespoons chili powder

2 tablespoons paprika

1 tablespoon mustard seeds

1 tablespoon coriander seeds

2 tablespoons kosher salt

2 tablespoons packed brown sugar

1 tablespoon garlic salt

2 teaspoons cayenne pepper

1 boneless prime rib beef roast,
   10 to 12 pounds

TO MAKE THE RUB: In a large sauté pan over medium-high heat, toast the cumin seeds, chili powder, paprika, mustard seeds, and coriander seeds, shaking the pan occasionally, until the spices start to smoke, about 2 to 3 minutes. Transfer the mixture to a mortar or coffee grinder. Add the salt, brown sugar, garlic salt, and cayenne. Grind the mixture coarsely.

Trim nearly all of the fat from the prime rib. Evenly spread the rub all over the prime rib. Cover with plastic wrap and refrigerate for at least 3 hours or as long as 12 hours.

Grill the prime rib, fat side up, indirectly over medium heat for about 2½ hours. Remove the prime rib when it reaches the desired doneness. Loosely cover the prime rib with aluminum foil and allow it to rest for 30 minutes before slicing, during which time the internal temperature will rise 5 to 10 degrees. Cut into slices ½ to 1 inch thick. Serve warm.

MAKES 12 TO 15 SERVINGS

WINE NOTES: *Even a highly seasoned prime rib will taste better with a red wine that's lighter than you'd pair with a T-bone or filet steak. Try a Spanish Rioja or an Italian Sangiovese.*

Santa Maria Tri-Tip Sandwich

Santa Maria, California, is home to the Barbecue Hall of Fame and a passionate band of grillers who have perfected the art of cooking a relatively unknown but unbelievably delicious cut of meat. Also known as "bottom sirloin butt," tri-tip should be grilled no more than medium-rare, then cut into thin slices and served on French bread.

INDIRECT/MEDIUM HEAT

FOR THE SAUCE:

- 1 tablespoon olive oil
- ½ cup finely diced red onion
- 1 teaspoon minced garlic
- ½ cup chicken broth
- ¼ cup ketchup
- ¼ cup steak sauce
- 1 tablespoon finely chopped fresh parsley
- 1 tablespoon Worcestershire sauce
- 1½ teaspoons ground coffee
- ¼ teaspoon freshly ground black pepper

FOR THE RUB:

- 1 tablespoon cracked black pepper
- 2 teaspoons garlic salt
- 1 teaspoon dry mustard
- 1 teaspoon paprika
- ¼ teaspoon cayenne pepper

- 2 to 2½ pounds tri-tip beef, about 1½ inches thick
- 12 slices French bread

Oak, mesquite, or hickory chips soaked in water for at least 30 minutes

TO MAKE THE BARBECUE SAUCE: In a medium saucepan over medium-high heat, warm the olive oil. Add the onion and garlic and cook, stirring occasionally, until soft, about 5 minutes. Add the chicken broth, ketchup, steak sauce, parsley, Worcestershire sauce, ground coffee, and black pepper. Bring the mixture to a boil, then reduce the heat to a simmer and cook, stirring occasionally, until reduced to ½ cup, about 10 minutes. Puree the sauce in a food processor or blender. Allow to cool, cover and refrigerate until ready to use. Bring to room temperature before serving.

To make the dry rub: In a small bowl, mix together the black pepper, garlic salt, mustard, paprika, and cayenne. Press the mixture into the surface of the tri-tip, cover with plastic wrap, and refrigerate for 3 hours or as long as 24 hours.

Follow the grill's instructions for using wood chips. Sear the tri-tip directly over medium heat, turning once, until both sides are seared, about 5 minutes total. Then grill the tri-tip indirectly over medium heat, turning once, until the internal temperature is about 140°F for medium-rare, 20 to 30 minutes more. Allow to rest for 5 minutes before slicing thinly on the diagonal against the grain.

Build each sandwich with slices of meat and a dollop of sauce. Serve warm or at room temperature.

MAKES 6 SERVINGS

WINE NOTES: *Look for a wine with lots of fruit and a bit of acid for balance: a Rhône-style blend from the home of the tri-tip, California's Central Coast.*

Beef Tenderloin with Spring Rolls

The unmistakable opulence of beef tenderloin gets a boost of flavor here from basil butter. Because the thin end of the tenderloin cooks much more quickly than the rest, trim that part off and use it for another recipe.

INDIRECT/HIGH HEAT

FOR THE PEANUT SAUCE:

¾ **cup dry-roasted peanuts**

½ **cup coconut milk**

¼ **teaspoon red curry paste**

1 **tablespoon each brown sugar, lime juice, and chopped fresh cilantro**

FOR THE BUTTER:

¾ **cup unsalted butter, softened**

½ **cup chopped fresh basil**

2 **tablespoons fresh lemon juice**

½ **teaspoon kosher salt**

¼ **teaspoon black pepper**

FOR THE SPRING ROLLS:

3-inch **piece seedless cucumber**

2 **medium carrots**

1 **red bell pepper, seeded**

1 **head baby bok choy**

2 **ounces rice sticks**

15 to 20 **fresh cilantro leaves**

15 to 20 **fresh mint leaves**

8 **rice-paper wrappers, 10 inches each**

1 **beef tenderloin, 4 to 5 pounds**

2 **teaspoons kosher salt**

1 **tablespoon cracked black pepper**
Vegetable oil for brushing meat

TO MAKE THE PEANUT SAUCE: In a food processor, grind the peanuts until as fine as cornmeal. In a medium saucepan, combine the peanuts, coconut milk, curry paste, brown sugar, lime juice, and ½ cup water. Bring to a boil, then reduce the heat to a simmer and cook, stirring occasionally, until the sauce is as thick as yogurt, 10 to 15 minutes. Stir in the cilantro.

To make the butter: In a small bowl, combine the butter, basil, lemon juice, salt, and pepper. Mix well.

To make the spring rolls: Peel the cucumber and carrots, then cut the cucumbers, carrots, and bell pepper into matchsticks and the bok choy into ⅛-inch-wide strips. Place in a large bowl. Cook the rice sticks in boiling water until tender, about 3 minutes. Drain and add to the bowl with the cilantro and mint leaves. Toss well. Brush both sides of each sheet of rice paper with hot water to soften. Place a small handful of the vegetable mixture on the bottom third of each sheet of rice paper. Fold the ends in and tightly roll up each sheet into a cylinder. Cut each cylinder in half on an angle.

Trim the thin end from the beef tenderloin and reserve for another use. Press the salt and pepper into the remaining meat. Lightly brush the tenderloin with vegetable oil. Sear directly over high heat, turning occasionally, until seared on all sides, 8 to 10 minutes. Then grill the tenderloin indirectly over high heat. The meat will take 30 to 40 minutes more to reach medium-rare. Remove from the grill and allow to rest for about 10 minutes, during which time the internal temperature will rise about 5 degrees.

Slice the tenderloin and serve with the basil butter. Serve the spring rolls with the peanut sauce.

MAKES 8 SERVINGS

WINE NOTES: *Here's another chance to show off that vintage Bordeaux or high-end California Cabernet you've been hoarding.*

Hamburgers of Their Dreams

When asked what makes the best burger, some people will defend their preferences with more than a little conviction. It seems that toppings are the most controversial, so lay out a plethora of choices. Ground chuck, which is 80 percent lean, tends to make the juiciest burgers. Ask your butcher to grind the meat fresh for you.

DIRECT/MEDIUM HEAT

4 to 6 slices bacon

6 to 8 medium white or brown mush-rooms, cut into ¼-inch-thick slices

2 large yellow or red onions, cut crosswise into ½-inch-thick slices

1½ tablespoons olive oil

1½ pounds ground beef chuck

½ teaspoon kosher salt

½ teaspoon freshly ground pepper
   Vegetable oil for brushing cooking grate

4 to 6 thin slices assorted cheeses (or equal amount crumbled)

8 slices French or Italian bread or 4 rolls, split, toasted if desired

1 large avocado, pitted, peeled, and cut into ¼-inch-thick slices

2 red or yellow tomatoes, cut cross-wise into ¼-inch-thick slices

1½ cups tomato salsa

3 ounces lettuce leaves or baby greens
   Ketchup
   Mustard

PLACE THE BACON IN A LARGE SAUTÉ PAN, put the pan over medium heat, and cook, turning often, until browned, 8 to 10 minutes. Transfer the bacon to paper towels to drain. Pour off all but 1 tablespoon of the fat from the pan. Raise the heat to medium-high, add the mushrooms, and cook, stirring occasionally, until tender, 5 to 6 minutes.

Lightly brush both sides of the onion slices with the olive oil. Grill directly over medium heat, turning once, until tender, 12 to 14 minutes total.

In a medium bowl, mix the meat with the salt and pepper. Form into 4 patties, each about ¾-inch thick. The burgers should be lightly shaped, as working them too hard will create an unappealing texture. Lightly brush the cooking grate with vegetable oil. Grill the burgers directly over medium heat, turning once, until no longer pink. Resist the urge to press down on the burgers during grilling, or you will force out the juices.

To make cheeseburgers, 3 to 4 minutes before the meat is done, place the cheese on top and allow it to melt. Serve warm on the bread with the bacon, mushrooms, onions, avocado, tomatoes, salsa, lettuce, ketchup, and mustard.

MAKES 4 SERVINGS

WINE NOTES: *A jammy red wine will match this burger-and-fixin's perfectly. Consider a Zinfandel, a ripe Beaujolais from a recent vintage, or a heady Côtes-du-Rhône or Vacqueyras from southern France. Don't be afraid to chill your selection for a short while beforehand.*

wine country lunch

In the summertime, in the great outdoors, the rules of lunch relax. Instead of successive courses, you have platters placed about the table. Instead of polite conversation, you hear loud laughter. For a palate cleanser, you turn to mineral water. And in place of pre-meal jitters, you've got easy anticipation, because a "wine country" lunch can be very simple. All you really need is a warm day, an outdoor spot, a group of good friends, and a sense of delight.

Begin with the setting. In the height of summer, seek the shade of an old oak tree—or an arbor, an umbrella, or an overhanging eave. Beneath it, set out a

table of cedar or teak, steel or cast iron. The top may be stone, glass, or battered wood—or an old door, laid across sawhorses, ready for service.

Drape the table in a Provençal print cloth, with matching or complementary napkins, and you create a carefree air. Old silverplate utensils add rustic charm; local fruit and flowers add native flavor. (Don't forget the decorative possibilities of squash blossoms. Just snip some flower-laden vines and use them as a tabletop garland.) As for the dishes, you can mix odd china patterns, or set out some good, sturdy bistro crockery.

For the wine, bring out several different bottles of chilled Sauvignon Blanc. Open and inviting,

the rules of lunch relax

crisp and refreshing, with hints of lemon and fresh-cut grass, this wine tastes like summertime. And this is no fussy tasting event, with notebooks and buckets and cubes of bread. Just sample one wine and then another until you find a favorite, then pour a full glass for the lunch to come.

It could be a Niçoise salad, ripe with fresh greens and rich with olives. Or generous cuts of halibut, bathed in a tomato-tarragon cream sauce. Or roast chicken still sizzling from the rotisserie, fragrant with the scents of garlic and mint.

To make your lunch easier, grill the chicken the day before. It tastes good straight from the fridge, sliced and tossed in a garden salad and served with crusty bread. For dessert, consider grilled peaches with homemade vanilla ice cream, or a berry crisp still warm from the grill.

The nice thing is, every one of these dishes is only a suggestion. When you're outdoors, a picnic atmosphere prevails, so you can feast on grapes or artichokes, fish or brisket. You can climb

the food pyramid or revel in a single food group. You might even take a two-hour trip to the land of pâté and sausage, cheese and chocolate. (Keep a hammock handy for the post-lunch nap.)

The key to lunch success? Prepare early. Don't fret. Take the time to savor a langorous meal in the sweet warmth of a summer afternoon. Above all, enjoy your guests. Listen to their laughter. Remember that if lunch is the main course, friendship is the dessert

Rosemary and Garlic Veal Chops with Grilled Mushrooms

Look for veal chops that are at least an inch thick. They maintain their juiciness and delicate flavors on the grill better than thinner chops. Be sure to pull them off the fire while their centers are still a little pink.

DIRECT/MEDIUM HEAT

- **2 tablespoons olive oil**
- **4 teaspoons finely chopped fresh rosemary**
- **2 teaspoons minced garlic**
- **1 teaspoon grated lemon zest**
- **½ teaspoon kosher salt**
- **¼ teaspoon freshly ground black pepper**
- **4 veal rib chops, each about ¾ pound and 1 inch thick**

FOR THE VEGETABLES:

- **½ pound fresh shiitake mushrooms, each 3 to 4 inches in diameter, stems removed**
- **1 yellow onion, cut crosswise into ½-inch-thick slices**
- **2 tablespoons olive oil**
- **Kosher salt**
- **Freshly ground black pepper**
- **1 small red tomato, seeded and cut into ⅓-inch dice**
- **1 small yellow tomato, seeded and cut into ⅓-inch dice**
- **1 tablespoon chopped fresh thyme**
- **2 teaspoons sherry vinegar**
- **1 tablespoon extra-virgin olive oil**

IN A SMALL BOWL, combine the olive oil, rosemary, garlic, lemon zest, salt, and pepper. Brush the mixture over both sides of the veal chops. Refrigerate the chops while you prepare the vegetables.

To make the vegetables: In a medium bowl, coat the shiitake mushrooms and onions with the 2 tablespoons olive oil. Season with salt and pepper to taste. Grill the mushrooms and onions directly over medium heat, turning once, until tender, 10 to 15 minutes. Remove the mushrooms and onions from the grill and allow them to cool, then cut into ½-inch pieces. Place in a medium bowl and add the red and yellow tomatoes and the thyme. Drizzle in the vinegar, then the 1 tablespoon extra-virgin olive oil. Mix well. Season with salt and pepper to taste.

Grill the veal chops directly over medium heat, turning once, until the centers are slightly pink and beads of juice are visible on the surface (the internal temperature should be about 150°F), about 20 minutes total.

Remove the veal from the grill and allow it to rest for 2 to 3 minutes. Serve warm with the vegetables.

MAKES 4 SERVINGS

WINE NOTES: *A medium-bodied red wine that balances fruit and acid is called for. A ripe Chianti from a good recent vintage (1997 was excellent), or a high-quality Barbera or Valpolicella.*

Citrus-Glazed Pork Tenderloin

Pork tenderloin is favored by grillers because it is so easy to move around the grill and it cooks quickly. If it has been marinated in a somewhat sweet-and-spicy mixture, such as this one, its expansive surface area takes on robust flavors and a glistening glaze.

INDIRECT/MEDIUM HEAT

FOR THE MARINADE:

2 tablespoons ketchup

2 tablespoons hoisin sauce

1 tablespoon rice wine vinegar

2 teaspoons grated orange zest

1 teaspoon hot chili sauce

1 teaspoon sesame oil

½ tablespoon soy sauce

1½ teaspoons curry powder

2 pork tenderloins, ¾ to
1 pound each

Vegetable oil for brushing
cooking grate

TO MAKE THE MARINADE: In a medium bowl, whisk together the ketchup, hoisin sauce, vinegar, orange zest, chili sauce, sesame oil, soy sauce, and curry. Add the tenderloins to the bowl and turn to coat well. Cover and refrigerate for 3 hours or as long as 8 hours.

Lightly brush the cooking grate with vegetable oil. Remove the tenderloins from the marinade, wiping off most of the marinade, and grill indirectly over medium heat, turning once, until the center is barely pink (the internal temperature should be 155°F to 160°F), 20 to 30 minutes.

Remove the tenderloins from the grill and carve into thick slices. Serve warm.

MAKES 4 SERVINGS

WINE NOTES: *Fruit, spice, and body are the keywords here. An Australian Shiraz would be a very good match indeed, or a Grenache blend from southern France or central California.*

Hoisin-Glazed Baby Back Ribs

Baby back ribs have less fat and cook more quickly than spare ribs. During the last half hour or so of grilling, baste the tender meat with this ginger-spiked hoisin sauce. For an attractive presentation, tie the ribs together in pairs with bok choy and scallions. They can be served as a starter or as a main course.

INDIRECT/MEDIUM HEAT

FOR THE GLAZE:

- 1 **cup hoisin sauce**
- ¼ **cup honey**
- ¼ **cup red wine vinegar**
- 2 **tablespoons grated fresh ginger**
- 1 **tablespoon minced garlic**
- 1 **tablespoon sesame oil**
- 2 **teaspoons curry powder**

- 4 **to 6 pounds pork baby back ribs**
-   **Kosher salt**
-   **Freshly ground black pepper**
- 1 **tablespoon sesame seeds**

TO MAKE THE GLAZE: In a small saucepan over medium heat, combine the hoisin sauce, honey, vinegar, ginger, garlic, sesame oil, and curry powder. Bring to a simmer, stirring occasionally, and cook over low heat for 2 to 3 minutes to blend the flavors. Remove from the heat.

Season the ribs liberally with salt and pepper. Grill indirectly over medium heat, turning halfway through the cooking time. When the ribs have cooked for 1 hour, start basting them every 15 minutes or so with the hoisin glaze until the meat is very tender and has shrunk from the ends of the bones, 15 to 30 minutes more. A few minutes before the ribs are finished, sprinkle them with the sesame seeds.

Remove the ribs from the grill and cut between the bones. Serve warm.

MAKES 4 TO 6 SERVINGS

WINE NOTES: *A fruity red—Gamay Beaujolais, young Zinfandel, or Australian Shiraz—will stand up to the sweetness and spice of the glaze on these succulent, slow-cooked ribs.*

Street-Corner Sausages
with Grilled Onions and Fennel

On busy street corners in big cities where people regularly eat on the run, hawkers with nothing but a grill, a pair of tongs, and a few basic ingredients make mouthwatering meals such as this one. Precooked or smoked sausages need only be warmed, while fresh sausages must be cooked until the insides are no longer pink.

DIRECT/MEDIUM HEAT

1 small fennel bulb

2 large yellow onions

1½ tablespoons olive oil

   Kosher salt

   Freshly ground black pepper

6 fresh sausages such as Italian, each 4 to 5 ounces and about 1¼ inches thick

6 hot dog buns or rolls, split

   About ½ cup spicy brown or coarse-grain mustard

CUT OFF THE STALKS AND OUTER LEAVES of the fennel bulb. Cut the bulb lengthwise into ½-inch-thick slices, keeping the root end attached to prevent the slices from falling apart. Cut the onions crosswise into ½-inch-thick slices. Lightly brush both sides of the fennel and onion slices with the olive oil. Season with salt and pepper to taste. Grill the slices directly over medium heat, turning once, until tender, 12 to 14 minutes. Remove from the grill and allow to cool. Cut away the bit of root from each fennel slice. Cut the fennel and onion slices into ½-inch pieces.

Grill the sausages directly over medium heat, turning once, until firm and no longer pink in the center, about 12 to 15 minutes. A few minutes before the sausages are cooked, toast the cut sides of the buns directly over medium heat.

Place each sausage inside a toasted bun. Add some grilled fennel and onions, and drizzle on some mustard. Serve warm.

MAKES 6 SERVINGS

WINE NOTES: *These simple sandwiches offer enough flavor for a wide range of wines to gain a foothold. A young, tannic red wine will work at one extreme; at the other, a fruity Chardonnay that's seen little or no oak.*

Boneless Pork Chops with Fire-Roasted Tomatillo Sauce

Tomatillos, a popular ingredient in the Mexican pantry, look like small green tomatoes with a papery husk. Grilling enhances their taste and softens their skin, making it possible to puree them for a sauce. Brining the pork chops is a tried-and-true technique for producing moist, evenly cooked meat.

DIRECT/MEDIUM HEAT

FOR THE MEAT:

- 2 tablespoons kosher salt
- 2 teaspoons ground cumin
- ½ teaspoon cayenne pepper
- 4 boneless pork chops, each 6 to 8 ounces and about 1 inch thick

FOR THE SAUCE:

- 8 medium tomatillos, husked and rinsed
- 1 poblano chile, 3 to 4 ounces
- 2 slices bacon
- 2 teaspoons minced garlic
- 1 white onion, about ½ pound, cut into ¼-inch dice
- 1 cup loosely packed fresh cilantro, without tough stems
- ½ teaspoon brown sugar
- ½ teaspoon kosher salt
- ¼ teaspoon freshly ground black pepper

Olive oil for brushing pork chops

TO BRINE THE MEAT: In a medium bowl, combine the salt, cumin, and cayenne with 2 cups water. Stir to dissolve the salt. Submerge the pork chops in the brine. Cover and refrigerate for 45 to 60 minutes.

To make the sauce: Grill the tomatillos directly over medium heat, turning occasionally, until blistered and soft, 6 to 8 minutes. Grill the poblano chile directly over medium heat, turning occasionally, until blistered but still holding its shape, 6 to 8 minutes. When the chile is cool enough to handle, remove and discard the skin, stem, and seeds.

In a medium sauté pan, cook the bacon over medium heat, turning occasionally, until crisp, about 10 minutes. Transfer the bacon to paper towels to drain. Add the garlic and onion to the fat remaining in the pan and cook over medium heat, stirring occasionally, until the onion is soft, about 4 minutes. Remove the pan from the heat.

In a food processor or blender, puree the tomatillos and chile. Add the bacon, garlic-onion mixture, cilantro, brown sugar, salt, and pepper. Process until smooth. Transfer to a medium sauté pan over low heat. Bring to a simmer. If the sauce seems too thick, stir in 2 to 3 tablespoons water. Taste for seasonings. Keep warm over low heat.

Remove the pork chops from the brine, pat dry with paper towels, and lightly brush both sides with olive oil. Grill the pork chops directly over medium heat, turning once, until barely pink in the center, 9 to 11 minutes total.

Serve the pork chops warm with the tomatillo sauce.

MAKES 4 SERVINGS

WINE NOTES: *Beer here! Look for a brew that's complex enough to complement the chiles in the sauce—one that can take a chill but retain its flavor. Try a Negra Modelo or Dos Equis—Mexican beers readily found in this country.*

Smoky Pulled Pork Sandwich

In North Carolina, debates over the best sauce for pulled pork have raged for decades. Some folks favor vinegar-based sauces, like the one presented here, while others insist on a mustard sauce and still others on a tomato-based one.

INDIRECT/LOW HEAT

FOR THE PORK:

2 tablespoons paprika

1 tablespoon each packed brown sugar, chili powder, ground cumin, and granulated sugar

2 teaspoons kosher salt

1½ teaspoons black pepper

1 boneless pork shoulder roast (Boston butt), 4 to 5 pounds

FOR THE COLESLAW:

1 head red cabbage, 1½ pounds

¼ cup cider vinegar

1 tablespoon granulated sugar

1 teaspoon each celery seeds and kosher salt

½ teaspoon black pepper

¾ cup mayonnaise

1 tablespoon Dijon mustard

FOR THE SAUCE:

½ cup cider vinegar

2 tablespoons brown sugar

½ teaspoon Tabasco sauce

1 teaspoon kosher salt

Hickory or mesquite chips, soaked in water for at least 30 minutes

TO PREPARE THE PORK: In a small bowl, mix together the paprika, brown sugar, chili powder, cumin, granulated sugar, salt, and pepper. Rub the mixture into the meat. Wrap the pork in plastic wrap and refrigerate for at least 3 hours or as long as 24 hours.

To make the coleslaw: Cut the cabbage in half through the core. Remove the core and slice the cabbage as thinly as possible. In a large bowl, mix together the vinegar, sugar, celery seeds, salt, pepper, mayonnaise, and mustard. Add the cabbage and toss to coat evenly. Cover and refrigerate for at least 1 hour or as long as 24 hours.

To make the sauce: In a medium saucepan over medium-high heat, combine the cider vinegar, brown sugar, Tabasco sauce, and salt. Bring the mixture to a boil. Reduce the heat to low and simmer for 10 minutes. Allow to cool to room temperature. Warm the sauce over low heat before serving.

Follow the grill's instructions for using wood chips. Grill the pork, fat side up, indirectly over low heat until very tender but still juicy (the internal temperature should be 180°F to 190°F), 3 hours or more. Remove the pork from the grill, cover it loosely with aluminum foil, and allow it rest for 30 minutes. Remove any skin from the meat. Tear the pork into shreds with two forks or your fingers. Put the shredded meat in a large bowl and toss with the warm vinegar sauce. Pile the pulled pork on hamburger buns and serve with coleslaw.

MAKES 10 TO 12 SERVINGS

WINE NOTES: *A dedicated wine lover might stumble on an ideal match here, but lemonade, root beer, or a frosty iced tea might be the best options.*

good Lamb marinade

Double-Cut Lamb Chops
with Cucumber-Yogurt Sauce

In Greek tavernas, a cucumber-yogurt sauce, tsatziki, *is commonly served, and its clean, bright flavors superbly complement the intensity of grilled lamb chops. You can use single lamb chops for this recipe, but double chops are preferred because you can grill them long enough to sear them well on the outside, yet still leave the center ruby red.*

DIRECT/MEDIUM HEAT

FOR THE SAUCE:

3-inch piece seedless cucumber,
   peeled and cut into ¼-inch dice

4 scallions, white parts only, minced

1 tablespoon fresh lemon juice

1 cup plain yogurt, nonfat if desired

1 tablespoon extra-virgin olive oil

1 tablespoon finely chopped fresh dill

⅛ teaspoon paprika

   Kosher salt

   Freshly ground black pepper

1 tablespoon fresh lemon juice

3 tablespoons extra-virgin olive oil

2 teaspoons finely chopped
   fresh oregano

2 teaspoons minced garlic

½ teaspoon kosher salt

¼ teaspoon freshly ground
   black pepper

8 double-cut rib lamb chops,
   1 to 1¼ inches thick, trimmed
   of nearly all fat

TO MAKE THE SAUCE: In a medium bowl, combine the cucumber, scallions, lemon juice, yogurt, olive oil, dill, and paprika. Mix well. Season with salt and pepper to taste.

In a small bowl, whisk together the lemon juice, olive oil, oregano, garlic, salt, and pepper. Brush the lamb chops with the olive oil mixture and allow to marinate at room temperature for 10 minutes.

Grill the lamb chops directly over medium heat, turning once. The chops will take about 10 minutes to reach medium-rare. Serve warm with the sauce.

MAKES 4 SERVINGS

WINE NOTES: *Consider a medium-bodied Pinot Noir from Oregon or Burgundy, and go easy on the cucumber-yogurt sauce if wine is a priority.*

Moroccan Butterflied Leg of Lamb

Moroccans use pungent spice blends to their best advantage, often toasting the dried seeds to release their aromas and then combining them with flavorful ingredients such as orange zest and garlic. In this recipe, the spices perfume the lamb as it cooks gently over indirect heat. An authentic accompaniment would be couscous with golden raisins.

DIRECT/MEDIUM HEAT

FOR THE PASTE:

2 teaspoons whole coriander seeds

2 teaspoons whole black peppercorns

½ teaspoon whole cloves

3 tablespoons minced garlic

Grated zest of 2 large oranges

1 teaspoon kosher salt

¼ cup olive oil

1 boneless leg of lamb, 3 to 4 pounds, butterflied

TO MAKE THE SPICE PASTE: In a medium sauté pan over medium-high heat, toast the coriander seeds, peppercorns, and cloves, shaking the pan occasionally, until the spices start to smoke, 2 to 3 minutes. Transfer the mixture to a mortar or coffee grinder and grind. Transfer to a small bowl and mix in the garlic, orange zest, salt, and olive oil.

Spread the leg of lamb flat. Trim the excess fat and sinew from the inside and outside. With the fat side facing down, use a sharp knife to make several horizontal slits at a 45-degree angle into the thickest parts of the lamb, until the meat is of even thickness. With a meat mallet or the bottom of a heavy pan, pound the lamb to an even thickness of about 1½ inches. Evenly spread the spice paste over both sides of the lamb. Wrap in plastic wrap and refrigerate for at least 1 hour or as long as 8 hours.

Grill the lamb, fat side down first, directly over medium heat, turning once. The lamb will take 15 to 25 minutes to reach medium-rare. Remove the lamb from the grill and let rest for 5 minutes before carving. Slice the meat on on a slight diagonal across the grain. Serve warm.

MAKES 6 TO 8 SERVINGS

WINE NOTES: *A Pinot Noir with real depth and character—and a bit of balancing acidity—would go nicely here. If the night is warm, try chilling it for a few minutes before serving.*

Provençal Rack of Lamb

The strength of Provençal home cooking depends largely on the combination of familiar, soulful flavors that culinary fashion can never improve. This plate of grilled lamb and white bean salad is a perfect illustration.

DIRECT/MEDIUM HEAT

FOR THE MARINADE:

1 small yellow onion

6 large garlic cloves, crushed

4 plum tomatoes, roughly chopped

½ cup each lightly packed fresh
 parsley and rosemary

2 tablespoons Dijon mustard

1 cup dry red wine

1 teaspoon kosher salt

½ teaspoon freshly ground pepper

FOR THE WHITE BEANS:

1 cup dried cannellini beans

4 cups chicken broth

1 small yellow onion, quartered

1 carrot, cut into 2-inch pieces

1 celery stalk, cut into 2-inch pieces

1½ teaspoons dried oregano

 Freshly ground black pepper

 Kosher salt

¼ cup extra-virgin olive oil

1 tablespoon red wine vinegar

2 tablespoons minced fresh parsley

1 cup fresh tomato, ½-inch dice

½ cup thinly sliced black or
 green olives

2 racks of lamb, 1½ to 2 pounds each

 Oil for brushing cooking grate

TO MAKE THE MARINADE: In a food processor, combine the onion, garlic, tomatoes, parsley, rosemary, mustard, red wine, salt, and pepper. Process until pureed, then pour into a large bowl. Trim any excess fat from the lamb and "french" the racks (cut the meat away from the ends of the ribs). Add the lamb to the bowl, turn to coat, cover, and refrigerate for 4 to 6 hours.

To make the white beans: In a large saucepan over high heat, combine the beans and 4 cups water and bring to a boil. Remove from the heat, cover, and let rest for 1 hour. Drain and rinse the beans, then return them to the saucepan with the chicken broth, onion, carrot, celery, and oregano. Season with pepper to taste. Bring the mixture to a boil, then lower the heat to a simmer and cook until the beans are tender, 1 to 1½ hours. During the last 10 minutes of cooking, season with salt to taste. Remove and discard the onion, carrot, and celery. Drain the beans and transfer them to a medium bowl. Add the olive oil, vinegar, parsley, tomato, and olives. Mix well. Taste for seasonings. Serve the white bean salad at room temperature.

Remove the lamb from the marinade. Cover the bones with aluminum foil to prevent them from burning. Lightly brush the cooking grate with vegetable oil. Grill the lamb directly over medium heat, turning once. The lamb will take 20 to 30 minutes to reach medium-rare. Let the lamb rest for 5 minutes before cutting it into chops. Serve warm with the white beans.

MAKES 4 SERVINGS

WINE NOTES: *Choose a Côtes-du-Rhône from a top vintage, or another red from southern France with equivalent fruit and body. Coteaux d'Aix-en-Provence and Côtes du Lubéron are two regions that pack both sunshine and value into their red wines.*

chicken & poultry

From India to Spain, Tuscany to Jamaica: As the recipes in this chapter prove, chicken may be the most international of foods. Here in the United States, we grill a lot of chicken, and with good reason. The lean, delicious meat is widely available, relatively inexpensive, and remarkably tender after just a short period of cooking.

In this chapter we share favorite marinades, sauces, and accompaniments that turn all sorts of poultry into classic international dishes. We include some tricks of the trade, including how to flatten a whole chicken and grill it under the weight of bricks to promote even cooking. We explain how to score the skin of duck breasts to control the amount of fat that drips from them and thus prevent flare-ups. And we point out how to secure your position as the undisputed hero of your next Thanksgiving meal—by using an apple-juice brine and wood smoke to produce a succulent, amber-colored turkey.

Butterflied Chicken under Bricks

Flattening a chicken under the weight of a brick may seem gimmicky, but the technique helps the meat to cook more evenly and promotes a crispier skin. The accompanying barbecue sauce, which tastes sweet and tangy at first, then builds slowly in heat, has authentic Kansas City character.

INDIRECT/HIGH HEAT

FOR THE BARBECUE SAUCE:

¼ **cup orange juice concentrate**

¼ **cup mild chili sauce**

2 **tablespoons dark molasses**

1 **tablespoon soy sauce**

2 **teaspoons whole-grain mustard**

1 **tablespoon white wine vinegar**

1 **teaspoon Worcestershire sauce**

½ **teaspoon Tabasco sauce**

½ **teaspoon kosher salt**

FOR THE CHICKEN:

2 **whole chickens, about 3 pounds each**

Kosher salt

Freshly ground pepper

Vegetable oil for brushing cooking grate

Nonstick cooking spray for greasing baking sheet

3 **bricks, wrapped in aluminum foil**

TO MAKE THE BARBECUE SAUCE: In a small saucepan, combine the orange juice concentrate, chili sauce, molasses, soy sauce, mustard, white wine vinegar, Worcestershire sauce, Tabasco sauce, and salt. Bring to a boil, then simmer for about 5 minutes. Remove from the heat and allow to cool to room temperature.

Place 1 chicken on a cutting board, breast side up. Position a heavy knife or poultry shears inside the cavity, and cut through the ribs along one side of the backbone. Make a second cut through the ribs along the other side of the backbone. Remove and discard the backbone. Turn the chicken over. With the heels of your hands, press down on the ribs and flatten the bird. Remove any bones that stick up. Repeat with the second chicken. Season both sides of the chickens with salt and pepper to taste.

Lightly brush the cooking grate with vegetable oil. Place the chickens, skin side down, over indirect high heat. Lightly coat the bottom of a baking sheet with cooking spray. Place the baking sheet on top of the chickens and weight it down with the bricks. Grill the chickens indirectly over high heat for 30 minutes. Using thick pot holders, remove the bricks and the baking sheet. If the skin is crispy and the juices run clear, the chickens are ready to serve. If not, continue to grill them indirectly over high heat, but without the baking sheet and bricks. Remove the chickens when the meat is opaque throughout and the juices run clear.

Cut the chickens into quarters. Serve warm with the barbecue sauce.

MAKES 4 TO 6 SERVINGS

WINE NOTES: *A full-bodied, fruity red such as a California Petite Sirah would go well here, or an amber ale with some sweetness of its own.*

Chicken Breasts with Fresh Tomato Salad and Oregano Oil

The age-old Italian tradition of making flavored oils takes only a few minutes and adds immeasurable character to both the chicken and the tomato salad. In place of oregano, other sturdy-leaved herbs such as rosemary or sage could be used alone or in combination to make oils to suit your particular fancy.

INDIRECT/MEDIUM HEAT

¼ **cup finely chopped fresh oregano**

½ **cup olive oil (not extra virgin)**

¼ **cup white wine vinegar**

2 **tablespoons Dijon mustard**

1 **tablespoon finely chopped fresh rosemary**

2 **tablespoons finely chopped garlic**

½ **teaspoon kosher salt**

¼ **teaspoon cayenne pepper**

2 **whole boneless chicken breasts**

1 **cup elbow macaroni**

2 **cups seeded, chopped tomatoes**

¾ **cup freshly grated Parmesan cheese**
   Freshly ground black pepper

IN A SMALL SAUCEPAN, combine the oregano and olive oil. Set the pan over high heat and cook until the leaves begin to sizzle. Cook for 10 seconds more, remove from the heat, and stir the oil until the sizzling stops. Strain through a fine-mesh sieve into a small bowl. Press the herbs with the back of a spoon to release every drop of flavor into the oil. Allow to cool to room temperature. (Covered and refrigerated, the oil will keep for up to a week.)

In a medium bowl, combine ¼ cup of the oregano oil with the vinegar, mustard, rosemary, garlic, salt, and cayenne pepper. Add the chicken breasts, turn to coat thoroughly, cover, and marinate in the refrigerator for at least 30 minutes or as long as 4 hours.

Bring a medium saucepan filled three-quarters with salted water to a boil. Add the macaroni and cook until al dente. Drain and place in a medium bowl. Add the tomatoes and cheese and toss well. Season with black pepper to taste. Add the remaining oregano oil and toss again.

Remove the chicken breasts from the marinade and place them, skin side down, over indirect medium heat. Grill, turning once, until the meat is opaque and the juices run clear, 10 to 12 minutes total.

Slice the chicken breasts and serve warm with the macaroni.

MAKES 4 SERVINGS

WINE NOTES: *The herb-infused oil suggests a white wine with some aroma and spice of its own, like a fresh, young Sauvignon Blanc or French Sancerre.*

Lemongrass and Curry Chicken Breasts with Fresh Tropical Salsa

Food in Indonesia is often aromatically extravagant because the local cooks generally fry their spices and other seasonings before applying them to meats. That extra step releases essential oils and flavors, which are apparent in this recipe. The tropical salsa makes a nice counterpoint.

INDIRECT/MEDIUM HEAT

FOR THE SALSA:

¾ cup finely diced ripe mango

½ cup finely diced ripe papaya

½ cup finely diced red bell pepper

½ cup finely diced seedless cucumber

½ cup finely diced red onion

1 tablespoon finely chopped fresh mint

1 to 2 teaspoons minced jalapeño chile, without the seeds

2 tablespoons fresh lime juice

½ teaspoon kosher salt

FOR THE CHICKEN:

2 stalks lemongrass

1-inch piece fresh ginger, peeled and thinly sliced

1 tablespoon hot chile sauce

1 tablespoon curry powder

2 tablespoons peanut oil, plus more for brushing cooking grate

1 tablespoon soy sauce

Juice of 1 lime

4 boneless chicken breast halves, skin on, 4 to 5 ounces each

TO MAKE THE SALSA: In a medium bowl, combine the mango, papaya, bell pepper, cucumber, red onion, mint, jalapeño, lime juice, and salt. Cover and refrigerate for at least 30 minutes or as long as 8 hours. Bring to room temperature before serving.

Cut away and discard any hard, dried parts of the lemongrass. Cut crosswise into ⅛-inch-thick slices. In a food processor or blender, combine the lemongrass, ginger, chile sauce, curry powder, and 2 tablespoons peanut oil. Puree until smooth. In a medium saucepan over medium-high heat, cook the pureed mixture until the aroma is apparent, about 5 minutes. Mix in the soy sauce, lime juice, and ¼ cup water. Allow to cool to room temperature.

Put the chicken breasts in a large bowl. Cover with the cooled pureed mixture. Toss to coat thoroughly. Cover and refrigerate for at least 1 hour or as long as 8 hours.

Lightly brush the cooking grate with peanut oil. Place the chicken breasts, skin side down, over indirect medium heat. Grill, turning once, until the meat is opaque throughout and the juices run clear, 10 to 12 minutes.

Serve the chicken breasts warm with the tropical salsa.

MAKES 4 SERVINGS

WINE NOTES: *A white wine with real fruit is required here: a semi-sweet Riesling, or a full-bodied Chardonnay from Australia or northern Italy.*

Smoked Chicken Risotto

The people living near the flatlands of northern Italy's Po River, where Arborio rice grows abundantly, cook risotto with authority. One way these cooks embellish the soul-satisfying qualities of risotto is by adding smoked chicken or pork. This entire recipe could be prepared on a grill, as long as you control the heat to simmer the rice gently.

INDIRECT/MEDIUM HEAT

- 1 tablespoon brown sugar
- 1½ tablespoons kosher salt
- ½ teaspoon freshly ground pepper
- 2 boneless chicken breast halves, skin on
- 5 ounces snow peas, trimmed
- 4 to 5 cups chicken stock
- ½ cup unsalted butter
- 1 teaspoon finely chopped garlic
- 1 yellow onion, finely diced
- 1¼ cups Arborio rice
- 2 bay leaves
- 2 tablespoons finely chopped fresh parsley
- ½ cup freshly grated Parmesan cheese

  Hickory chips, soaked in water for 30 minutes

IN A SMALL BOWL, mix together the sugar, salt, and pepper. Coat the chicken breasts evenly with the mixture, put them in a medium bowl, cover, and refrigerate for at least 2 hours or as long as 6 hours.

Follow the grill's instructions for using wood chips. Place the chicken breasts, skin side down, over indirect medium heat. Grill, turning once, until the meat is opaque throughout and the juices run clear, 10 to 12 minutes total. Remove from the grill and thinly slice the chicken.

Bring a medium saucepan filled three-quarters with salted water to a boil. Add the snow peas and parboil until barely tender, about 3 minutes. Drain and immediately cool under cold running water. Drain again and cut into ½-inch pieces.

In a small saucepan, bring the chicken stock to a simmer. In a large saucepan over medium heat, melt half of the butter. Add the garlic and onion and cook, stirring occasionally, until they are soft, about 5 minutes. Add the rice and stir until the grains are coated with butter. Add about ½ cup of the simmering stock and the bay leaves and simmer, stirring continuously, until the rice absorbs almost all of the liquid. Add another ½ cup of the stock. Continue to stir until the rice absorbs the liquid. Continue adding stock and stirring until the rice is almost tender, about 25 minutes total. Remove the bay leaves. Add the parsley, cheese, and the remaining butter along with the chicken and snow peas. Stir and cook only enough to mix in the ingredients and warm them. Season with salt and pepper to taste. Serve immediately.

MAKES 4 SERVINGS

WINE NOTES: *A well-structured white wine with the acidity to refresh the palate between bites, such as a Napa Valley Fumé Blanc, balances the richness of this dish.*

GOOD!

Tandoori Chicken Pieces

Originating in the Punjab region of northwestern India, tandoori dishes refer to foods that have been marinated in a mixture of tangy yogurt and aromatic spices, and then roasted in a clay oven called a tandoor. _The flavors also come alive in the circulating heat of a hot grill. Use drumsticks if you are serving appetizers; for a main course, breasts and legs work best. A cucumber salad and flatbread are traditional accompaniments._

INDIRECT/MEDIUM HEAT

FOR THE MARINADE:

2 cups (1 pint) plain yogurt

1 tablespoon grated fresh ginger

1 tablespoon minced garlic

2 teaspoons paprika

2 teaspoons kosher salt

1½ teaspoons ground cinnamon

1 teaspoon ground cumin

1 teaspoon ground coriander

½ teaspoon freshly ground pepper

¼ teaspoon ground cloves

3 pounds chicken pieces, bone in
Vegetable oil for brushing cooking grate

TO MAKE THE MARINADE: In a large bowl, combine the yogurt, ginger, garlic, paprika, salt, cinnamon, cumin, coriander, pepper, and cloves. Mix well and set aside.

Rinse the chicken pieces and pat dry. Using a sharp knife, make ½-inch-deep scores in the chicken meat at 1-inch intervals. Add the chicken pieces to the marinade and coat well, working the marinade into the cuts. Cover and refrigerate for at least 8 hours or as long as 12 hours.

Lightly brush the cooking grate with vegetable oil. Scrape most of the marinade from the chicken pieces. Grill them indirectly over medium heat, turning occasionally, until the meat is opaque throughout and the juices run clear. Breasts will take about 45 minutes, while drumsticks will take about 1 hour. Serve warm.

MAKES 6 SERVINGS

WINE NOTES: _Spicy but not hot, these chicken pieces can be enjoyed with a variety of straightforward wines, both white and red. Beer lovers will do nicely with an English-style ale._

Garlic-and-Mint-Roasted Chicken

Tuscan restaurants called girarrosti *(roasting spits) serve this style of simple, hearty food all day long, often from wood-burning fireplaces situated right in the dining room, where guests can admire the slowly revolving chickens, pork roasts, and game of all types. An outdoor grill equipped with a rotisserie will achieve the same magnificent results. Don't have a rotisserie? No worries. Just place the chicken on the cooking grate and grill over indirect medium heat.*

INDIRECT/HIGH HEAT

10 to 12 medium garlic cloves

1½ cups lightly packed fresh mint leaves

1 tablespoon chili powder

1 teaspoon kosher salt

½ teaspoon freshly ground pepper

¼ cup olive oil

¼ cup fresh orange juice

2 tablespoons soy sauce

1 whole chicken, 4 to 5 pounds

IN A FOOD PROCESSOR OR BLENDER, combine the garlic, mint, chili powder, salt, pepper, olive oil, orange juice, and soy sauce. Puree until smooth. Remove the wing tips and excess fat from the chicken. Spread the puréed mixture all over the outside and inside of the chicken. Truss the chicken with cotton string. Place in a plastic bag, secure closed, and marinate in the refrigerator for 8 hours or as long as 24 hours.

Following the grill's instructions, secure the chicken in the middle of a rotisserie, put the rotisserie in place, and turn it on. Cook the chicken indirectly over high heat until the juices run clear and the internal temperature of the breasts is 170°F, 1 to 1¼ hours. Check the chicken occasionally; if the skin is browning too quickly, reduce the heat slightly.

When the chicken is fully cooked, turn off the rotisserie and, using thick pot holders, remove the rotisserie from the grill. Slide the chicken from the rotisserie, being careful not to splatter yourself with the hot juices. Cut the chicken into serving pieces. Serve warm.

MAKES 4 SERVINGS

WINE NOTES: *Toast this dish with a crisp, uncomplicated Tuscan wine such as Vernaccia di San Gimignano—served in small tumblers.*

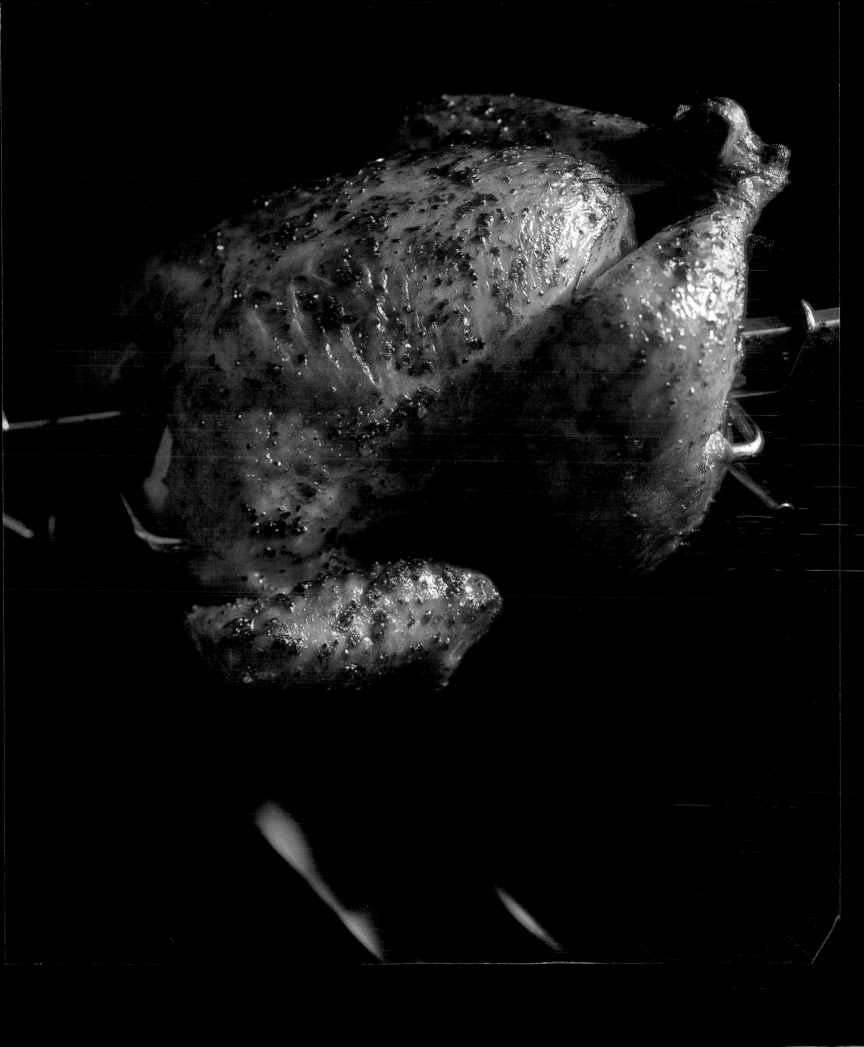

Jackson's Jerk Chicken

A beach at the northeastern end of Jamaica, where this recipe hails from, is home to a huge rectangular pit that is covered with a grate and filled with wood coals crackling with pimento branches. Grilling guru Chris Jackson rubs chicken pieces with a paste of brutally hot Scotch bonnet chiles and other seasonings before cooking them slowly on the grill and turning them frequently. He recommends a hefty dose of allspice for a true taste of jerk cooking.

INDIRECT/MEDIUM HEAT

FOR THE PASTE:

14 scallions, including the tender green parts, finely chopped

2 Scotch bonnet chiles, including seeds, finely chopped

⅓ cup red wine vinegar

3 tablespoons soy sauce

1½ tablespoons hot-pepper sauce, preferably coarse, yellow Trinidad style

½ cup ground allspice

2 tablespoons grated fresh ginger

¼ teaspoon grated nutmeg

1 teaspoon ground cinnamon

2 tablespoons vegetable oil

1 tablespoon kosher salt

1 teaspoon coarsely ground pepper

FOR THE CHICKEN:

8 whole chicken legs, bone in

Juice of 3 limes

1 tablespoon kosher salt

Vegetable oil for brushing cooking grate

TO MAKE THE PASTE: In a food processor or blender, combine the scallions, Scotch bonnet chiles, vinegar, soy sauce, hot-pepper sauce, allspice, ginger, nutmeg, cinnamon, vegetable oil, salt, and pepper. Puree until smooth.

Place the chicken legs in a large bowl and rub them with the lime juice and salt. Pour the paste over the chicken legs and rub it into the meat with your fingers. (Since the chiles are extremely hot, you may choose to wear rubber gloves when handling them.) Cover and refrigerate the legs for at least 8 hours or as long as 24 hours.

Lightly brush the cooking grate with vegetable oil. Grill the chicken legs indirectly over medium heat, turning occasionally, until the meat is opaque throughout and the juices run clear, about 40 minutes. Serve warm.

MAKES 8 SERVINGS

WINE NOTES: *Even wine-lovers will reach for a cold beer (or two) with these fiery treats. The spices will blend well with a Belgian-style lambic beer. Or to be authentic, reach for a Red Stripe Jamaican lager.*

Paella Valencia

Paella originated in Valencia, along the east coast of Spain, and was traditionally cooked in a wide, shallow pan above a live fire—a technique you can conveniently approximate with a sauté pan and a grill. If you are up for the challenge of attempting this recipe on a charcoal grill, set up your grill for indirect cooking.

DIRECT/HIGH HEAT

- 4 ounces green beans, trimmed
- 4 ounces pork tenderloin, cut into 1-inch cubes
- 4 ounces chorizo sausage, cut into ½-inch-thick slices
- 2 boneless chicken thighs, cut into 1-inch pieces
- 3 garlic cloves, thinly sliced
- 4 ounces squid, cleaned and cut into ¼-inch-wide rings, tentacles left whole
- 1¼ cups Arborio rice
- 4 to 5 cups chicken stock
- 1 cup diced tomato (½-inch dice)
- ⅓ cup diced roasted red bell pepper (½-inch dice)
- Pinch saffron threads
- 2 teaspoons paprika, preferably Spanish
- 1 tablespoon finely chopped fresh thyme
- 1 bay leaf
- Kosher salt
- Freshly ground pepper
- 6 to 10 medium shrimp, peeled and deveined
- 6 to 10 mussels, scrubbed and debearded

BRING A SMALL SAUCEPAN filled three-quarters with salted water to a boil. Add the green beans and cook until tender-crisp, about 3 minutes. Drain and immediately cool under cold running water. Drain again and cut into 1-inch pieces. Set aside.

In a 10- to 12-inch paella pan or a similar ovenproof sauté pan placed on the cooking grate directly over high heat, brown the pork tenderloin and chorizo sausage on all sides, 6 to 8 minutes. Remove the pork tenderloin and sausage, add the chicken, and brown on all sides, 5 to 6 minutes. Remove the chicken and add the garlic and squid and cook, stirring occasionally, until the garlic browns, about 2 minutes.

Add the rice and stir until the grains are coated with fat. Return the pork, chorizo, and chicken to the pan. Add 4 cups of the chicken stock, the tomato, roasted pepper, saffron, paprika, thyme, and bay leaf. Season with salt and pepper to taste. Stir well.

Bring to a boil, then move the pan over indirect low heat. Simmer, without stirring, until most of the liquid has been absorbed and the rice is almost tender, 20 to 25 minutes. (If all the liquid is absorbed before the rice is tender, add another ½ to 1 cup chicken stock or water and cook for an additional 5 to 10 minutes until absorbed.) Remove the bay leaf. Add the shrimp, mussels, and green beans, pushing them a bit below the surface. The ends of the mussels that will open should face up. Continue to cook indirectly over low heat until the shrimp are opaque and the mussels are open, 5 to 7 minutes. Discard any mussels that do not open. Carefully remove the pan from the grill and let rest for 5 minutes before serving.

MAKES 4 SERVINGS

WINE NOTES: *A white Rioja would be both authentic and delicious with this dish. As an alternative, try a chilled Rhône-style rosé (Grenache or Counoise) from France or California.*

Apple-Brined and Hickory-Smoked Turkey

For many grillers, producing a juicy, amber-colored turkey imbued with wood smoke is a benchmark of pride. An apple juice-based brine and 24 hours of marination are the keys to this uncommonly tasty version.

INDIRECT/MEDIUM HEAT

FOR THE BRINE:

2 quarts apple juice

1 pound brown sugar

1 cup kosher salt

3 oranges, quartered

4 ounces fresh ginger, thinly sliced

15 whole cloves

6 bay leaves

6 large cloves garlic, crushed

1 turkey, 12 to 14 pounds
Vegetable oil for brushing turkey

Cotton string for trussing turkey
Roasting rack
Heavy-gauge foil pan

Hickory chips, soaked in water for at least 30 minutes

IN A LARGE SAUCEPAN over high heat, bring the apple juice, brown sugar, and salt to a boil, stirring to dissolve the sugar and salt. Cook for 1 minute, remove from the heat, and skim off the foam. Allow the mixture to cool to room temperature.

In a 5-gallon plastic bucket or other container large enough to easily hold the turkey, combine 3 quarts of water, the oranges, ginger, cloves, bay leaves, and garlic. Add the apple juice mixture and stir.

Remove and discard the fat from the turkey cavity. Reserve the neck and giblets for another use. Rinse the turkey inside and out, drain, and submerge the turkey in the brine. If necessary, top with a heavy weight to make sure it is completely immersed. Refrigerate for 24 hours.

Follow the grill's instructions for using wood chips. Set up the grill for indirect cooking over medium heat.

Remove the turkey from the brine and pat with paper towels until very dry. Tie the legs together with cotton string. Lightly brush the turkey with vegetable oil, and place on a roasting rack set inside a heavy-gauge foil pan. Cook indirectly over medium heat. When the wings are golden brown, about 40 minutes, wrap them with aluminum foil to prevent them from burning. Brush the rest of the turkey with vegetable oil. When the turkey breasts are golden brown, about 1 hour, cover the turkey with aluminum foil to prevent the skin from getting too brown. The turkey is done when its juices run clear, the internal temperature of the thickest part of the thighs is about 180°F, and the internal temperature of the breast is about 165°F. Figure 12 to 14 minutes per pound.

Transfer the turkey to a cutting board or platter, cover loosely with aluminum foil, and let rest for 20 minutes before carving. The pan drippings may be used to make gravy.

MAKES 12 TO 15 SERVINGS

WINE NOTES: *The lightly smoked meat pairs especially well with a Chardonnay-based Macon Blanc from France, or a spicy Gewürztraminer. Red-wine lovers would do well with a Châteauneuf-du-Pape.*

Turkey Drumsticks Slathered with Barbecue Sauce

There's really no better way to eat one of these big clubs of dark, flavorful turkey than to clench it with a tight fist and tear the meat with your teeth. The secret to preparing juicy turkey drumsticks on the grill is to baste them with a low-sugar sauce such as the one offered here. If you use a sweeter sauce, baste only during the last 15 minutes to avoid burning the drumsticks.

INDIRECT/MEDIUM HEAT

FOR THE SAUCE:

  2 **tablespoons olive oil**

  ½ **cup finely chopped red onion**

  2 **garlic cloves, finely chopped**

  ¼ **cup dry red wine**

  ¼ **cup ketchup**

  ¼ **cup steak sauce**

1½ **tablespoons Worcestershire sauce**

  1 **teaspoon dried sage**

  ½ **teaspoon freshly ground pepper**

  Vegetable oil for brushing cooking grate

  4 **turkey drumsticks, about 1 pound each**

TO MAKE THE SAUCE: In a medium saucepan over medium-high heat, warm the olive oil. Add the onion and garlic and cook, stirring occasionally, until soft, about 5 minutes. Add the red wine, ketchup, steak sauce, Worcestershire sauce, sage, and pepper. Bring to a boil, reduce the heat to a simmer, and cook for 5 minutes. Remove from the heat.

Lightly brush the cooking grate with vegetable oil. Lightly coat the turkey drumsticks with the barbecue sauce. Grill the drumsticks indirectly over medium heat, turning and basting with the barbecue sauce every 30 minutes, until the juices run clear and the internal temperature is 180°F, 1½ to 2 hours. Serve warm.

MAKES 4 SERVINGS

WINE NOTES: *A lightly chilled and fruity red wine is a good match: a rustic Beaujolais-Villages or its New-World equivalent, Gamay Beaujolais.*

Crispy Asian Duck Breasts and Soft Polenta

Preparing duck breasts on the grill can be a challenge because of their higher fat content—unless you know a little secret. By trimming and scoring the skin, the fat is rendered gradually, so flare-ups don't occur. Prepared this way, you can even use direct heat.

DIRECT/LOW HEAT

- 2 teaspoons Chinese five-spice powder
- 1 teaspoon kosher salt
- ½ teaspoon freshly ground pepper
- 4 boneless duck breast halves, 7 to 8 ounces each

FOR THE POLENTA:

- 3 cups vegetable or chicken stock
- ¾ cup finely ground yellow cornmeal
- ⅓ cup sour cream
  Kosher salt
  Freshly ground pepper

FOR THE SAUCE:

- ¼ cup ketchup
- ¼ cup hoisin sauce
- 1 tablespoon honey
- 2 tablespoons rice wine vinegar
- 1 tablespoon soy sauce
- ¼ teaspoon Chinese five-spice powder

WITH A SHARP KNIFE, trim the skin on the duck breasts to a thickness of ¼ inch. Remove any skin or fat that hangs over the edge. Score the skin of each duck breast at ½-inch intervals, but do not cut into the flesh. In a small bowl, mix together the five-spice powder, salt, and pepper. Lightly coat both sides of the duck breasts with the seasonings.

To make the polenta: In a large saucepan, bring the stock to a boil. Pour the cornmeal into the stock in a thin stream, whisking constantly to avoid lumps. Reduce the heat to low and cook, stirring occasionally with a wooden spoon to prevent scorching, for 30 to 45 minutes. Stir in the sour cream. Season with salt and pepper to taste. Keep warm over low heat. Stir in more stock or water, if necessary, to maintain a soft consistency.

To make the sauce: In a small saucepan, stir together the ketchup, hoisin sauce, honey, rice wine vinegar, soy sauce, and the Chinese five-spice powder. Bring to a simmer over low heat just prior to serving.

Place the duck breasts, skin side down, on the cooking grate, grilling them directly over low heat until the skin is golden brown and crisp, 7 to 8 minutes. Turn and grill until they are as firm to the touch as the heel of your hand (for medium-rare), 6 to 7 minutes more.

Remove the breasts from the grill. Allow to rest for 3 to 4 minutes. Slice thinly on the bias. Serve warm with the sauce and the polenta.

MAKES 4 SERVINGS

WINE NOTES: *Pinot Noir is the classic pairing for duck, although the sweetness of hoisin and ketchup may be better balanced by a Merlot.*

fish & seafood

The finer points of grilling fish and seafood have been passionately pursued from tropical beaches to chic urban grills, but certain techniques work no matter where you are.

First, clean your cooking grate thoroughly to prevent the fish from sticking. A light coating of cooking oil on both the grate and the fish is also helpful to prevent sticking, but be careful because too much oil may cause flare-ups. Firm-fleshed fish such as salmon, sea bass, swordfish, and tuna hold together particularly well on the grill. To know when a fillet is perfectly cooked (most often, at the point when the center is just changing from translucent to opaque), cut it open and peek. Once it's done, press the fillet with your finger and try to remember its resistance. After a while, you'll be able to check for doneness just by touch.

Shellfish such as shrimp, oysters, and lobster also cook fabulously on the grill. They require little if any oil, they take only a few minutes, and they leave little behind to clean. Whenever possible, grill them with the shells on to retain their flavorful juices.

Cedar-Planked Salmon

A full side of salmon presented on the cedar on which it was grilled makes an impressive statement. One-inch cedar boards can be found at most building supply stores, where they are often sold as fencing material. Be absolutely sure the wood is untreated before using it for cooking.

INDIRECT/HIGH HEAT

  1 **untreated cedar plank (about 16 inches by 8 inches)**

  1 **whole salmon fillet, skin on, 2½ to 3 pounds and about 16 inches long**

  ¼ **cup white wine**

   Finely shredded zest and juice of 1 lemon

  ⅓ **cup finely chopped fresh dill**

  1 **tablespoon kosher salt**

1½ **teaspoons freshly ground pepper**

IN A CONTAINER LARGE ENOUGH to hold the plank, immerse the plank in water for 1 hour or longer (you may need to weight it down). Lift the plank from the water and rinse it.

Place the salmon fillet, skin side down, on a baking sheet with sides. In a small bowl, mix together the white wine, lemon zest, lemon juice, dill, salt, and pepper. Pour the mixture over the salmon. Cover the salmon with plastic wrap and refrigerate for 30 minutes.

Uncover the salmon and place it, skin side down, in the middle of the plank. Cook the salmon (on the plank) indirectly over high heat until just opaque at the thickest part, 30 to 40 minutes. The internal temperature should be about 125°F.

Serve warm or at room temperature.

MAKES 8 TO 10 SERVINGS

WINE NOTES: *A bright, zippy Sauvignon Blanc will match the citrus in the marinade, while balancing the salmon's inherent richness. An offbeat alternative: a Viognier from California or Virginia.*

Herb-Crusted Salmon with Lentil Salad

Something extraordinary happens when fresh herbs in an olive oil–based paste meet the searing heat of a grill. They turn smoky and create an earthy crust for salmon or any firm-fleshed fish. For the salad, look for small French green lentils. They hold their shape well during cooking and have a highly distinctive taste.

DIRECT/MEDIUM HEAT

FOR THE SALAD:

- 2 tablespoons fresh lemon juice
- 3 tablespoons extra-virgin olive oil
- 3 dashes Tabasco sauce
- ¼ cup chopped fresh basil
- 2 scallions, thinly sliced
- ½ teaspoon kosher salt
- ¼ teaspoon freshly ground pepper
- ¾ cup French green lentils
- ⅓ cup quick-cooking couscous
- 2 roasted red bell peppers, finely diced
- 1 carrot, finely diced

FOR THE SALMON:

- 2 tablespoons finely chopped fresh parsley
- 2 tablespoons finely chopped fresh cilantro
- 2 tablespoons finely chopped fresh basil
- 1 teaspoon chili powder
- ½ teaspoon kosher salt
- ½ teaspoon coarsely ground pepper
- 4 tablespoons olive oil
- 1 teaspoon soy sauce
- 6 salmon fillets, skin on, each 6 to 7 ounces and 1 inch thick

TO MAKE THE SALAD: In a medium bowl, whisk together the lemon juice, olive oil, Tabasco, basil, scallions, salt, and pepper. Remove any small stones from the lentils. Rinse the lentils under cold running water, then put them in a medium saucepan with 3 cups water. Bring to a boil, then simmer until the lentils are tender, 25 to 30 minutes. Drain the lentils and add them to the olive oil mixture. In a small saucepan, bring ½ cup water to a boil. Place the couscous in a small bowl. Pour the boiling water over the couscous, stirring briefly with a fork. Cover and let stand for 5 minutes to absorb the water. Fluff gently with a fork. Add the couscous to the lentils. Add the bell peppers and carrots. Stir and toss to mix well. Adjust the seasonings, if necessary.

Combine the parsley, cilantro, and basil in a small bowl. Add the chili powder, salt, pepper, olive oil, and soy sauce. Mix thoroughly to create a paste. Evenly spread the paste over the flesh of the salmon fillets.

Place the salmon fillets, flesh side down, directly over medium heat. Grill, turning once, until just opaque at the thickest part, 10 to 12 minutes total. If desired, cut each salmon fillet in half to serve.

Serve warm with the lentil and couscous salad.

MAKES 6 SERVINGS

WINE NOTES: *Pepper and citrus provide any wine with a challenge—one readily met by a Sauvignon/Sémillon blend.*

Salmon with Brown Sugar
and Mustard Glaze

Grilling salmon on a piece of aluminum foil eliminates any chance of it sticking to the grate. In fact, you can close the lid knowing you don't even need to flip the fish. Once the sweet-and-sour glaze has caramelized on the fish, simply slide a spatula between the skin and flesh and serve.

INDIRECT/MEDIUM HEAT

1 tablespoon brown sugar

1 teaspoon honey

2 teaspoons unsalted butter

2 tablespoons Dijon mustard

1 tablespoon soy sauce

1 tablespoon olive oil

2 teaspoons grated fresh ginger

1 whole salmon fillet, skin on, about 2½ pounds and ¾ to 1 inch thick

IN A SMALL SAUTÉ PAN over medium heat, melt the brown sugar with the honey and butter. Remove from the heat and whisk in the mustard, soy sauce, olive oil, and ginger. Allow to cool.

Place the salmon, skin side down, on a large sheet of aluminum foil. Trim the foil to leave a border of ¼ to ½ inch around the edge of the salmon. Coat the flesh of the salmon with the brown sugar mixture.

Grill the salmon indirectly over medium heat until the edges begin to brown and the inside is opaque, 25 to 30 minutes. The internal temperature should be about 125°F. Turn off the heat and serve fish directly from the grill or, using a large baking sheet, carefully transfer the salmon with the foil to a cutting board. Cut the salmon crosswise into 6 to 8 pieces, but do not cut through the skin. Slide a spatula between the skin and flesh and remove the salmon pieces to a serving platter or individual plates. Serve immediately.

MAKES 6 TO 8 SERVINGS

WINE NOTES: *A ripe Pinot Noir gives an impression of sweetness to complement the glaze on this salmon, yet it will stand up to the rich fish and the spicy mustard.*

Jalapeño-Citrus Tuna Steaks

The availability of fresh tuna steaks at many supermarkets offers grill chefs a delicious new entrée. Grilling, in turn, is the best cooking method for this tender, red flesh, which is better just seared and rare rather than cooked to well done.

DIRECT/MEDIUM HEAT

FOR THE TUNA:

- 3 tablespoons olive oil
- 2 tablespoons finely chopped fresh oregano
- ½ teaspoon cayenne pepper
- 1 teaspoon kosher salt
- 4 ahi tuna steaks, each 7 to 8 ounces and 1 inch thick

FOR THE RELISH:

- 4 small oranges, about 6 ounces each
- 1 lime
- 1 teaspoon honey
- 1 jalapeño chile, seeded and minced
- 1 teaspoon red pepper flakes
- ⅛ teaspoon ground cumin

IN A SMALL BOWL, mix together the olive oil, oregano, cayenne pepper, and salt. Brush the mixture over both sides of the tuna steaks. Cover with plastic wrap and marinate in the refrigerator for at least 15 minutes or as long as 45 minutes.

To make the relish: With a sharp knife, cut the skin and outer white pith from the oranges. Slide the knife down one side of each orange segment, then down the other side, removing the segments as you go. Cut the segments into ½-inch pieces and place them in a bowl. Follow the same procedure for the lime and combine with the orange pieces. Add the honey, jalapeño chile, red pepper flakes, and cumin. Stir and toss to mix well.

Grill the tuna steaks directly over medium heat, turning once, for 4 minutes total for rare or as long as 8 minutes total for well done.

Serve warm with the citrus relish.

MAKES 4 SERVINGS

WINE NOTES: *A full-bodied, oak-aged Chardonnay with upfront fruit is the ticket here. A good red-wine alternative would be a young California Syrah.*

Halibut with Tomato-Tarragon Cream Sauce

The concentrated flavors of grilled tomatoes and onions plus the punch of sun-dried tomatoes impart a robust character to this simple sauce. A little goes a long way to perk up a mild-tasting fish like halibut. Be careful not to overcook the fish; it is rather lean and dries out easily.

DIRECT/MEDIUM HEAT

FOR THE SAUCE:

½ **yellow onion**

3 **plum tomatoes**

1 **tablespoon olive oil**

  Kosher salt

  Freshly ground pepper

3 **sun-dried tomatoes**

½ **cup boiling water**

¼ **cup heavy cream**

1 **tablespoon sherry vinegar**

1 **tablespoon roughly chopped fresh tarragon**

FOR THE HALIBUT:

4 **halibut fillets, each 7 to 8 ounces, about 1 inch thick**

2 **tablespoons olive oil**

  Kosher salt

  Freshly ground pepper

TO MAKE THE SAUCE: Cut the onion half crosswise into ½-inch-thick slices. Core the tomatoes and cut crosswise into ½-inch-thick slices. Brush the onion and tomato slices with the olive oil. Season with salt and pepper to taste. Grill the onion slices directly over medium heat, turning once, until soft, 12 to 14 minutes total. Grill the tomato slices directly over medium heat, turning once, until grill marks are clearly visible, 8 to 10 minutes total.

Place the sun-dried tomatoes in a bowl and add the boiling water. Allow to soften for about 15 minutes. Remove the sun-dried tomatoes, reserving the water. Place the sun-dried tomatoes in a food processor along with the grilled onions and tomatoes. With the processor running, add the cream, vinegar, and tarragon. Add enough of the reserved water to make a smooth sauce. Season with salt and pepper to taste. Transfer to a small saucepan and keep warm over low heat.

Brush the halibut fillets with the olive oil. Season with salt and pepper to taste. Grill the halibut fillets directly over medium heat, turning once, until the flesh just begins to flake when tested with a fork, about 8 minutes total.

Serve warm with the sauce.

MAKES 4 SERVINGS

WINE NOTES: *Look Loire-ward: An off-dry Vouvray will match the roasted onion and the cream, while a top-notch Sancerre will complement the tarragon and sherry vinegar.*

Sea Bass en Papillote

The French term en papillote *refers to food cooked enclosed in paper, usually parchment, which traps steaming juices and aromas. Here, succulent sea bass simmers in a covered foil container with a heady broth of white wine, butter, and shallots mixed with the natural juices of the fish.*

INDIRECT/MEDIUM HEAT

- 1 **whole sea bass, about 2 pounds, cleaned and scaled, or 4 fillets, about ½ pound each**
- ½ **cup dry white wine**
- ½ **cup finely diced fresh mushrooms**
- 2 **tablespoons unsalted butter**
- 2 **tablespoons finely chopped shallots**
- 2 **medium garlic cloves, thinly sliced**
- 1 **tablespoon finely chopped fresh rosemary**
- 1 **bay leaf**
- ½ **cup diced tomatoes (½-inch dice)**
  Kosher salt
  Freshly ground pepper

PLACE THE SEA BASS in a foil pan large enough to hold the whole fish (or 4 fillets) easily. Distribute the wine, mushrooms, butter, shallots, garlic, rosemary, and bay leaf evenly around the fish. Cover tightly with heavy-duty aluminum foil.

Place the pan on the cooking grate over indirect medium heat. Cook until the flesh just begins to flake when tested with a fork, 25 to 30 minutes (or 10 to 15 minutes, depending on the thickness of the fillets).

Transfer the sea bass to a serving platter and keep warm. Pour the mixture from the foil pan into a small saucepan. Remove the bay leaf. Add the tomatoes, place over high heat, and simmer for 2 to 3 minutes. Season with salt and pepper to taste.

Pour the sauce over the sea bass. Serve warm.

MAKES 4 SERVINGS

WINE NOTES: *The rosemary, garlic, and tomato sing of the Mediterranean —which is why a light, refreshing wine with some acidity, like a Provençal rosé, is an excellent choice.*

Mahi-Mahi BLT

Mahi-mahi is a relatively mild-tasting fish, so it tastes best accompanied by strong flavors, such as those in the classic American bacon, lettuce, and tomato sandwich. Its firm, moist nature makes it an ideal fish for the grill.

DIRECT/MEDIUM HEAT

⅔ **cup mayonnaise**

⅓ **cup finely chopped yellow onion**

2 **tablespoons fresh lime juice**

½ **teaspoon paprika**

¼ **teaspoon freshly ground pepper**

4 **slices bacon, cut in half crosswise**

2 **tablespoons olive oil**

1 **tablespoon chili powder**

1 **tablespoon finely chopped garlic**

4 **mahi-mahi fillets, skin on, each about 8 ounces, 1 inch thick**

Vegetable oil for brushing cooking grate

8 **slices sourdough bread, each ½ inch thick**

4 **romaine lettuce leaves**

8 **thin tomato slices**

IN A SMALL BOWL, whisk together the mayonnaise, onion, lime juice, paprika, and pepper. Cover and refrigerate until needed.

In a medium sauté pan over medium-low heat, cook the bacon, turning often, until browned, 8 to 10 minutes. Transfer to paper towels to drain.

In a small bowl, whisk together the olive oil, chili powder, and garlic. Brush on the flesh side of the mahi-mahi fillets. Lightly brush the cooking grate with vegetable oil. Place the fillets, flesh side down, directly over medium heat and grill, turning once, until just opaque, 10 to 12 minutes total. Remove the skin before serving.

When the fish is almost cooked, grill the bread slices directly over medium heat until lightly toasted, about 2 minutes per side. Evenly spread one side of each bread slice with the mayonnaise mixture. Build each sandwich with 2 slices of bread, 1 lettuce leaf, 2 tomato slices, 2 half slices of bacon, and a mahi-mahi fillet.

Serve the sandwiches while the fish is still warm.

MAKES 4 SERVINGS

WINE NOTES: *We tried several white and red wines with this sandwich, but found nothing that worked as well as an ice-cold, slightly sweet lemonade.*

Caribbean Swordfish Steaks
with Mango Salsa

Rum, lime juice, and mangoes conjure up sultry evenings in the West Indies. Swordfish works well with these flavors, and because of its firm flesh, is perhaps the easiest of all fish to grill. Here, the marinade works twice: first to flavor the fish, then to keep it moist as it cooks.

DIRECT/MEDIUM HEAT

FOR THE SWORDFISH:

¼ cup olive oil

Juice of 4 limes

2 tablespoons rum

2 tablespoons soy sauce

¼ teaspoon ground cloves

¼ teaspoon freshly ground pepper

4 swordfish steaks, each 7 to 8 ounces, 1 inch thick

FOR THE SALSA:

1 large mango, about 1 pound, peeled, pitted, and cut into ½-inch dice

2 teaspoons thinly sliced scallions, white part only

1 jalapeño chile, seeded and finely chopped

1 tablespoon finely chopped fresh basil

1 teaspoon fresh lime juice

IN A MEDIUM BOWL, whisk together the olive oil, lime juice, rum, soy sauce, cloves, and pepper. Add the swordfish steaks and coat thoroughly. Cover and marinate in the refrigerator for 30 minutes or as long as 4 hours. Turn the swordfish halfway through marinating.

To make the mango salsa: In a small bowl, combine the mango, scallions, jalapeño chile, basil, and lime juice. Toss gently to mix.

Remove the swordfish steaks from the marinade. Pour the marinade into a small saucepan. Bring to a boil, then remove from the heat.

Grill the swordfish steaks directly over medium heat, brushing once with the boiled marinade and turning once, until just opaque, 10 to 12 minutes total.

Serve the steaks warm with the mango salsa.

MAKES 4 SERVINGS

WINE NOTES: *A full-bodied Chardonnay with citrus and tropical-fruit notes matches this recipe's rum, clove, mango, and lime juice.*

Apple-and-Leek-Stuffed Trout with Brown Butter Sauce

Pink, richly flavored trout flesh paired with this simple stuffing and butter sauce makes for a sumptuous feast. All the better if your fish is freshly caught. A recipe to take with you to the river.

DIRECT/MEDIUM HEAT

FOR THE STUFFING:

2 tablespoons unsalted butter

1½ cups thinly sliced leeks, including tender green parts

1½ cups finely diced green apple

1 tablespoon fresh lemon juice

2 teaspoons finely chopped fresh tarragon

½ teaspoon kosher salt

¼ teaspoon freshly ground pepper

FOR THE TROUT:

4 cleaned whole trout, 9 to 10 ounces each

2 tablespoons olive oil

Kosher salt

Freshly ground pepper

5 tablespoons unsalted butter

Juice of 1 lemon

3 tablespoons capers, rinsed

TO MAKE THE STUFFING: In a large sauté pan over medium heat, melt the butter. Add the leeks and cook, stirring occasionally, until tender, about 3 minutes. Add the apple and cook for 1 minute. Stir in the lemon juice, tarragon, salt, and pepper. Cook for 1 more minute. Remove from the heat and allow the stuffing to cool slightly.

Rinse the trout and pat dry. Fill each trout cavity with about ⅓ cup of the stuffing. Close the openings securely with wooden toothpicks. Lightly brush the trout with olive oil. Season with salt and pepper to taste. Grill the trout directly over medium heat, turning once, until just opaque, 12 to 14 minutes.

Meanwhile, in a medium saucepan over medium-high heat, melt the butter until it begins to brown, 3 to 4 minutes. Add the lemon juice and capers. Season with salt and pepper to taste. Keep the sauce warm over low heat, but don't let the butter burn.

Remove the toothpicks from the trout. Serve warm with the sauce spooned over the top.

MAKES 4 SERVINGS

WINE NOTES: *The tangy sauce and the herbal-citrus notes in the stuffing call for a wine with similar qualities—a straightforward California or New Zealand Sauvignon Blanc with little or no oak.*

SETTINGS:
city lights

Romance is more of a feeling than a thing, more the product of serendipity than it is of design. It might seem that planning a romantic dinner is well, unromantic. But the fact is, planning for romance is not merely acceptable in a busy world, it's essential. If you schedule an evening with your beloved, and block it out in ink, it rekindles commitment. And if you surprise someone with a meal that you've made from scratch, you regain the delight of discovery.

For starters, pick a good place. In warm weather, there's nothing like a rooftop hideaway or a sheltered patio, with a table set with candles—preferably in hurricanes or votive holders to shelter them from breezes. For dishes, use the best you have. The same goes for stemware, glasses, and silverware. If you've got some silver salt and pepper shakers, polish them up and bring them out. If you've got a good tablecloth and napkins, of linen or jacquard-woven cotton, use them. Or, for a more casual

look that's still beautiful, get some placemats in a fine weave or unusual material.

Flowers are crucial. Get out your best vase and fill it with your love's favorite flowers, or float a single blossom in a bowl of water.

For the meal itself, keep things simple. Salmon and swordfish are ideal on the grill and beautiful on the plate. Alongside, you might serve some wild rice, plus four or five stems of grilled asparagus, topped with a dab of hollandaise sauce. If this meal sounds too easy to be special, feel free to create something more elaborate. But remember that simplicity is the essence of elegance—and the main idea here is to enjoy a good meal in one another's company, not to fuss over a soufflé.

the essence of elegance

For a beverage, you might try a crisp Chardonnay, a perfumed Marsanne, or a delicate Pinot Noir. Better yet, serve a brut Champagne. It works with virtually any meal, and of course its very presence makes the evening a special event.

When the time comes for dessert, try a strawberry mousse. It's easy to make and wonderful to look at, and its bright, fresh flavors make a delicious counterpoint to the smoky notes of grilled salmon or swordfish.

Whatever you serve, and wherever you serve it, remember that a romantic evening is special mainly because you took the time to prepare it. Chances are, whatever you serve will taste fabulous, and will certainly be appreciated.

As for the timing, don't wait for a birthday or anniversary or holiday. While those days are fine, they are often loaded with expectation and obligation. Better to choose a date at random, and turn what might have been an ordinary evening into an extraordinary memory. When it comes to romance, the best occasion is "just because."

Diablo Shrimp and Angel Hair Pasta

Prepare to get messy. The best way to eat these fiery shrimp is to peel back the shells with your fingers and let the buttery juices run. Grilling with the shells on captures the natural moisture, leaving you succulence and spice. Serve with plenty of napkins.

DIRECT/HIGH HEAT

½ cup unsalted butter

1 tablespoon finely chopped garlic

1 teaspoon cayenne pepper

½ cup dry white wine

4 tablespoons finely chopped
   fresh parsley

1 pound jumbo shrimp (about 16),
   deveined but not peeled

½ teaspoon kosher salt

8 ounces angel hair (capellini) pasta

¼ cup extra-virgin olive oil

⅓ cup freshly grated Parmesan cheese

1 lemon, halved

IN A SMALL SAUCEPAN over medium heat, combine the butter, garlic, and cayenne pepper. Cook until the garlic is soft, about 5 minutes. Add the wine, raise the heat to high, and cook until reduced by half. Allow to cool. Stir in 2 tablespoons of the parsley.

Place the shrimp in a medium bowl. Pour the butter mixture over the shrimp. Add the salt. Toss the shrimp to coat them thoroughly.

Place the shrimp directly over high heat and grill, turning once, until just opaque, 3 to 4 minutes total. If flare-ups occur, temporarily move the shrimp away from the flame, positioning them over indirect heat.

Meanwhile, bring a saucepan full of salted water to a boil. Add the pasta and cook until al dente. Drain and toss with the olive oil, cheese, and the remaining 2 tablespoons parsley.

Transfer the shrimp to a bowl and squeeze the juice from the lemon halves over them. Toss well and serve immediately with the pasta.

MAKES 4 SERVINGS

WINE NOTES: *This is an easy match—serve with any young white wine (easy on the oak, or none at all) that can take a thorough chilling without losing its fruit.*

Lemon-Dill Shrimp
with Grecian Orzo Salad

This recipe is meant for warm summer days when we look for light, vibrant flavors to revive our spirits. The salad has a tangy intensity that complements the smoky flavor that only a grill can deliver to shrimp.

DIRECT/HIGH HEAT

FOR THE VINAIGRETTE:

- 1 teaspoon grated lemon zest
- ¼ cup fresh lemon juice
- ½ cup olive oil
- 1 tablespoon finely chopped fresh dill
- 1 teaspoon minced garlic
- ½ teaspoon kosher salt
- ¼ teaspoon freshly ground pepper

FOR THE SALAD:

- 16 jumbo shrimp (about 1 pound), peeled and deveined
- 1 cup orzo pasta
- 2 ounces feta cheese, crumbled
- ¾ cup finely diced red bell pepper
- ⅓ cup pitted kalamata olives, quartered
- 2 tablespoons thinly sliced scallions, including tender green parts
- 1½ tablespoons finely chopped fresh oregano

- 4 metal skewers (or bamboo skewers soaked in water for at least 30 minutes)

TO MAKE THE VINAIGRETTE: In a small bowl, whisk together the lemon zest, lemon juice, olive oil, dill, garlic, salt, and pepper. Place the shrimp in a medium bowl. Pour ¼ cup of the vinaigrette over the shrimp and toss to coat thoroughly. Cover with plastic wrap and marinate in the refrigerator for about 30 minutes.

Bring a medium saucepan three-quarters full of salted water to a boil. Add the pasta and cook until al dente. Drain and place in a bowl. Add the remaining vinaigrette and the feta cheese and toss well. Add the bell pepper, kalamata olives, scallions, and oregano. Toss again.

Thread 4 shrimp onto each skewer, bending each shrimp almost in half so that the skewer passes through it twice. Place the shrimp directly over high heat and grill, turning once, until just opaque inside with lightly browned edges, 4 to 5 minutes total.

Serve the shrimp immediately with the pasta.

MAKES 4 SERVINGS

WINE NOTES: *A fresh, crisp Pinot Gris will match well with the herbaceous notes of the dill and oregano, the creamy tang of the feta, and the briny kalamata olives.*

Smoky Lobster Tails and Corn on the Cob

Ah, the unmistakable luxury of grilled lobster tails. It's hard to believe they're so simple to make. If you use skewers, the tails will not curl while cooking. Grilled sweet corn and pure drawn butter make this a summertime favorite.

INDIRECT/MEDIUM HEAT

- 1 **cup (8 ounces) unsalted butter**
- 4 **ears of corn, in husks and silks trimmed**
- 4 **lobster tails, about ½ pound each**
  Kosher salt
  Freshly ground pepper

- 8 **metal skewers (or bamboo skewers soaked in water for at least 30 minutes)**

IN A SMALL SAUCEPAN over medium-high heat, melt the butter until foam rises to the top and the milk solids settle at the bottom. Remove from the heat. Using a spoon, carefully skim off the foam. Pour the clarified (drawn) butter into another small saucepan, being careful to leave behind the milk solids. Keep warm over low heat.

Place the corn in a deep container, cover with cold water and soak at least 1 hour. Remove the corn from the container; shake to remove excess water. Grill the corn indirectly over medium heat for 25 to 30 minutes, turning several times. Use gloves to remove husks and silk.

Place each lobster tail, shell side down, on a cutting board. Using a sharp knife or kitchen shears, cut lengthwise through the center of the tough underside of the tail, but do not cut into the flesh. Thread two skewers lengthwise through the flesh of each tail. Brush the flesh lightly with some drawn butter. Season with salt and pepper to taste.

Grill, shell side down, directly over medium heat just until the flesh turns opaque and the shell is bright red, 10 to 12 minutes.

Using a large knife, split each lobster tail lengthwise through the shell to better expose the flesh. Serve warm with the corn and the remaining drawn butter.

MAKES 4 SERVINGS

WINE NOTES: *Enjoy a rich, moderately oaked but only lightly chilled Chardonnay with the buttery, smoky lobster.*

Grilled Scallops with Fresh Pea Sauce

Large sea scallops grill up superbly. The fire gives them a golden caramelized exterior, while leaving the interior soft and creamy. A purée of sugar snap peas—edible pod and all—scented with tarragon makes a colorful, yet delicately flavored backdrop for these seafood gems.

DIRECT/MEDIUM HEAT

FOR THE SAUCE:

1 **pound sugar snap peas, ends trimmed**

2 **tablespoons extra-virgin olive oil**

2 **tablespoons roughly chopped fresh tarragon**

  Kosher salt

  Freshly ground pepper

  Juice of 1 lemon

3 **tablespoons sour cream**

FOR THE SCALLOPS:

12 **large sea scallops**

  Olive oil for brushing scallops

  Kosher salt

  Freshly ground pepper

1 **large tomato, seeded and finely diced**

4 **metal skewers (or bamboo skewers soaked in water for at least 30 minutes)**

TO MAKE THE PEA SAUCE: Bring a large saucepan filled three-quarters with salted water to a boil. Add the sugar snap peas and boil until soft, 7 to 8 minutes. Drain, reserving the water, and cool immediately in ice water. Drain again. In a food processor or blender, puree the peas with 1 cup of the cooking water, the olive oil, and the tarragon. Add more water, if necessary, to make a smooth sauce. Season with salt and pepper to taste. Warm the sauce in a small saucepan over medium heat. Add the lemon juice just before serving.

Thread 3 scallops through their sides onto each skewer so the scallops lie flat. Brush the scallops with olive oil. Season with salt and pepper to taste. Grill the scallops directly over medium heat, turning once, until just opaque, 4 to 5 minutes total.

Divide the sauce among 4 plates. Spoon single teaspoons of sour cream into the sauce and use the tip of a small knife to draw the sour cream through the sauce. Slide the scallops off the skewers and place them in the sauce. Garnish with the diced tomato.

MAKES 4 SERVINGS

WINE NOTES: *A rich white Burgundy, a natural partner to grilled scallops, has enough character to stand up to the sour cream and tarragon.*

Seared Calamari with Napa Cabbage Slaw

The sweet, nutty character of calamari is increasingly popular among today's chefs, but it takes practice to cook it right. Lightly scoring calamari before setting it on a hot grill and pulling it off when it's barely done ensures its tenderness.

DIRECT/HIGH HEAT

FOR THE SLAW:

¼ cup rice wine vinegar

2 teaspoons honey

6 tablespoons extra-virgin olive oil

3 scallions, including tender green parts, thinly sliced on the diagonal

2 teaspoons finely chopped fresh ginger

1 teaspoon caraway seeds

Kosher salt and freshly ground pepper

1 small head Napa cabbage

2 red bell peppers

3-inch length seedless cucumber

FOR THE CALAMARI:

3 tablespoons fresh lemon juice

2 tablespoons peanut oil

1 tablespoon Asian sesame oil

1 teaspoon soy sauce

3 dashes Tabasco sauce

1 tablespoon minced fresh cilantro

1 teaspoon each minced garlic and grated fresh ginger

1 teaspoon kosher salt

Freshly ground pepper

1½ pounds calamari (squid), each about 4 inches long, cleaned

TO MAKE THE SLAW: In a large bowl, combine the vinegar, honey, 2 tablespoons of the olive oil, the scallions, ginger, caraway seeds, and ½ teaspoon each salt and pepper. Cut the cabbage in half through the core. Cut the red bell peppers in half through the core, remove and discard the seeds, and flatten the peppers with the palm of your hand. Brush the cabbage and bell peppers with the remaining 4 tablespoons olive oil. Season with salt and pepper to taste.

Grill the cabbage and bell peppers directly over high heat until nicely browned, about 5 to 7 minutes. Allow the vegetables to cool. Remove the core of the cabbage. Cut the cabbage crosswise into ⅛-inch-thick slices. Cut the bell pepper into ⅛-inch-wide strips. Cut the cucumber into ⅛-inch-thick slices. Add the cabbage, bell peppers, and cucumbers to the dressing and toss well. Cover and refrigerate for as long as 2 days. Bring to room temperature before serving.

To make the calamari: In a bowl, combine the lemon juice, peanut oil, sesame oil, soy sauce, Tabasco sauce, cilantro, garlic, ginger, salt, and pepper to taste. With the tip of a sharp knife, lightly score the outside of the calamari (on both sides) in a crosshatch pattern, but do not cut all the way through. Add the calamari to the bowl, cover with plastic wrap, and marinate in the refrigerator for 45 to 60 minutes.

Thread the calamari onto metal or bamboo skewers (soak the latter for at least 30 minutes) to prevent them from curling as they grill. Transfer the marinade to a small saucepan over high heat. Bring the marinade to a boil, then remove from the heat. Grill the calamari directly over high heat, turning once and brushing once with the boiled marinade, until just firm and white, 2 to 3 minutes total.

Serve the calamari immediately with the slaw.

MAKES 4 SERVINGS

WINE NOTES: *A German Riesling or California Gewürztraminer will match the sweetness of the honey and grilled vegetables in the slaw.*

vegetable main dishes

Anyone who knows what a hot grill can do with the sweetness of freshly picked corn on the cob, or the fragrance of late-summer tomatoes, or the meaty texture of portobello mushrooms understands the rewards of cooking vegetables over flames. In this chapter, we combine the smoky, concentrated flavors of grilled vegetables with heftier ingredients like pasta, polenta, and breads to present a broad range of robust, meatless meals that could become classics in your home. We've given you reliable cooking times and temperatures, but the more you grill the better you'll understand when it's best to leave the vegetables crisp and barely kissed by the grill, and when they benefit from full-force fire-roasting. If your tomatoes seem soft, for example, you'll know to cut them a little wider next time so that they hold their shape. If your mushrooms feel moist, you'll raise the heat to speed up evaporation and sear them while retaining good texture. The road to great grilled vegetables is paved with experimentation.

Eggplant Stacks
with Roasted Corn Vinaigrette

To save time, roast the corn and red bell pepper for the vinaigrette at the same time that you draw out the bitter juices from the eggplant with salt. If you grill the eggplant a few hours before your guests arrive, all that is left to do is to assemble the stacks and warm them just before serving.

DIRECT/MEDIUM HEAT

FOR THE VINAIGRETTE:

1 **ear of corn, unshucked**

1 **red bell pepper**

2 **tablespoons finely chopped shallots**

2 **tablespoons balsamic vinegar**

2 **tablespoons coarsely chopped fresh basil**

5 **tablespoons extra-virgin olive oil**

8 **medium tomato slices, each ¼ inch thick**

   Kosher salt

   Freshly ground pepper

FOR THE EGGPLANT:

12 **globe eggplant slices, each about 4 inches in diameter and ½ inch thick**

   Kosher salt for rubbing eggplant

   Olive oil for brushing eggplant

   Freshly ground pepper

½ **cup grated or sliced Asiago cheese**

TO MAKE THE VINAIGRETTE: Soak the corn in water for 10 minutes. Grill the corn directly over medium heat, turning occasionally, until the husk is completely charred, 15 to 18 minutes. Remove and discard the charred husk and the inner silks. Remove the kernels with a sharp knife and place them in a medium bowl. Grill the bell pepper directly over medium heat, turning occasionally, until the skin is completely black and blistered, 10 to 12 minutes. Transfer the pepper to a paper bag, seal tightly, and let cool for 15 minutes. Remove the pepper, discard the skin and seeds, and finely dice. Add the bell pepper to the corn along with the shallot, vinegar, basil, olive oil, and tomato slices. Season with salt and pepper to taste. Make sure the tomatoes are covered by the vinaigrette.

Meanwhile, rub both sides of the eggplant slices thoroughly with salt. Allow them to sit in a colander placed in the sink or over a plate for about 30 minutes to draw out the bitter juices. Rinse well and pat dry. Brush thoroughly with olive oil and season with salt and pepper.

Grill the eggplant slices directly over medium heat, turning once, until tender, 10 to 12 minutes.

To assemble the stacks, start with an eggplant slice. Top with 1 tablespoon of the cheese and then a marinated tomato slice. Repeat the layers, ending with an eggplant slice. Carefully place the stacks on a small baking sheet. Place on the cooking grate directly over medium heat and cook until the cheese melts, 2 to 3 minutes.

Place the stacks on individual plates. Spoon the vinaigrette on top and around the sides. Serve warm.

MAKES 4 SERVINGS

WINE NOTES: *A light red wine with good acidity is called for: A young Italian Barbera d'Asti or Sangiovese di Romana is perfect.*

Fettuccine with Grilled Radicchio and Roquefort Cheese

The ripe, salty flavors of Roquefort cheese and the bitterness of radicchio and endive combine to make a rare treat for those who appreciate their distinctive qualities. Grilling the vegetables intensifies their earthiness, making the final dish more rustic than refined.

INDIRECT/MEDIUM HEAT

- ½ cup walnut pieces
- 3 heads Belgian endive
- 1 small head radicchio
- 3 tablespoons olive oil
- 6 ounces Roquefort or other blue-veined cheese
- 3 tablespoons walnut oil
- 2 tablespoons red wine vinegar
- 10 ounces fettuccine
- ¼ cup finely chopped fresh parsley
  Freshly ground pepper

IN A MEDIUM SAUTÉ PAN over medium heat, toast the walnuts, turning occasionally to avoid burning, until they just start to brown, about 10 minutes. Set aside.

Cut the Belgian endives in half lengthwise. Cut the radicchio in half through the core. Brush the Belgian endive and radicchio pieces with the olive oil. Grill them indirectly over medium heat, turning once, until lightly charred, 8 to 10 minutes total. Remove the vegetables from the grill and allow to cool. Cut the endives crosswise into ¼-inch-thick slices. Remove the core from the radicchio, discard the charred outer leaves, and cut the remaining leaves into ¼-inch-wide ribbons.

In a large bowl, combine the cheese, walnut oil, and red wine vinegar. Using the back of a fork, mash the ingredients together.

Bring a large saucepan full of salted water to a boil. Add the fettuccine and cook until al dente. Drain and add to the bowl with the Roquefort cheese mixture.

Add the Belgian endive, radicchio, walnuts, and parsley. Toss to combine thoroughly. Season with pepper to taste. Serve warm.

MAKES 4 SERVINGS

WINE NOTES: *Sweet wine with pasta? Focus on the* fromage, *not on the noodles, and you'll see the point of serving Chenin Blanc-based wine from the Loire Valley—a honeyed Vouvray or Montlouis.*

Vegetable Main Dishes

Polenta with Black Bean Salad and Green Chile Sauce

A toothsome black bean salad creates the perfect counterpoint to the supple texture of grilled polenta, while a pleasantly fiery green chile sauce ties the Mexican flavors together. This is a satisfying meal that even meat eaters will applaud.

DIRECT/HIGH HEAT

FOR THE POLENTA:

- 2 cups coarse yellow cornmeal
- 1 teaspoon kosher salt
- ½ teaspoon freshly ground pepper
- 2 tablespoons unsalted butter
- ¼ cup heavy cream

FOR THE SALAD:

- 1½ cups drained, cooked black beans
- ⅓ cup finely diced white onion
- ½ cup finely diced carrot
- ½ cup finely diced roasted red bell pepper
- Juice of 1 lime
- 3 tablespoons extra-virgin olive oil
- ½ teaspoon kosher salt
- ¼ teaspoon freshly ground pepper
- ¼ teaspoon ground cumin
- ¼ cup finely chopped fresh cilantro

Vegetable oil for brushing polenta

Green Chile Sauce (page 20)

TO MAKE THE POLENTA: In a large, heavy saucepan, combine the cornmeal with 6 cups water, the salt, and the pepper and whisk until smooth. Whisking constantly, bring the mixture to a boil over high heat and boil for 2 minutes. Reduce the heat to a simmer. Add the butter and cream, incorporating them with a wooden spoon. Allow to cook at a simmer until tender, 30 to 40 minutes, stirring every 5 minutes or so to avoid scorching. Transfer the polenta to a small baking pan and smooth the surface with a spatula dipped in water. The polenta should be about ½ inch thick. Allow to cool to room temperature. Cover and refrigerate until firm, at least 4 hours or as long as 24 hours.

To make the salad: In a medium bowl, combine the black beans, onion, carrot, and roasted pepper. In a small bowl, whisk together the lime juice, olive oil, salt, pepper, and cumin. Pour the vinaigrette over the bean mixture and mix together. Add the cilantro and mix again.

Cut the polenta into squares or other desired shapes. Brush both sides with vegetable oil. Grill directly over high heat, turning once, until warmed through, about 8 minutes total.

Serve the polenta warm with the black bean salad and Green Chile Sauce (see page 20).

MAKES 4 SERVINGS

WINE NOTES: *A fruity California Zinfandel for the wine lovers, and a pale ale for those who believe beer and chiles are meant for each other.*

Zucchini, Scallion, and Sun-Dried Tomato Frittata

What to do with leftover vegetables that you've grilled the night before? Combine them with well-seasoned eggs and cheese to make this delicious frittata. Of course you can also use fresh vegetables hot off the grill.

DIRECT/MEDIUM HEAT

5 tablespoons olive oil

1½ tablespoons balsamic vinegar

1 teaspoon finely chopped garlic

1 teaspoon kosher salt

½ teaspoon freshly ground pepper

1 zucchini, about 8 ounces, ends trimmed and sliced lengthwise ¼ inch thick

15 scallions, tough green ends trimmed

10 sun-dried tomatoes, softened in hot water to cover for 15 minutes, drained, and finely chopped

½ cup dried bread crumbs

4 ounces Teleme or Taleggio cheese, cut into ½-inch pieces

2 tablespoons finely chopped fresh basil

8 eggs

IN A MEDIUM BOWL, whisk together 4 tablespoons of the olive oil, the balsamic vinegar, garlic, ½ teaspoon of the salt, and ¼ teaspoon of the pepper. Add the zucchini and scallions and toss well. Grill the zucchini directly over medium heat, turning once, until tender, 8 to 10 minutes total. Grill the scallions directly over medium heat, turning occasionally, until lightly charred, about 4 minutes total. Cut the zucchini into ½-inch pieces. Cut the scallions into 1-inch lengths, discarding the root ends. Combine the zucchini, scallions, and tomatoes in a medium bowl.

Preheat the oven to 300°F.

In a sauté pan over medium-high heat, toast the bread crumbs with the remaining 1 tablespoon olive oil until golden, about 5 minutes. Stir often to avoid burning. Add half of the bread crumbs to the zucchini mixture. Set the other half aside. Add the cheese, basil, and the remaining ½ teaspoon salt and ¼ teaspoon pepper to the zucchini mixture. Toss all the ingredients together.

In another medium bowl, beat the eggs until blended, then add them to the vegetable mixture. Mix well and pour into an ovenproof 10-inch nonstick sauté pan (or use an ovenproof 10-inch sauté pan lined with parchment paper).

Bake the frittata for 15 minutes. Sprinkle the top evenly with the reserved bread crumbs, and continue to bake until a knife inserted in the center comes out clean, 5 to 10 minutes longer. Allow to cool for 10 minutes before removing from the pan.

Serve warm or at room temperature.

MAKES 6 SERVINGS

WINE NOTES: *Try an Italian Pinot Grigio if using a mild Teleme or Taleggio cheese, or an earthier variation (such as a Pouilly-Fumé) if the cheese has more character.*

Vegetable Main Dishes

Portobello Mushroom and Goat Cheese Sandwich

The portobello mushroom, with its large, suede cap, dense texture, and earthy flavor make it a favorite of grilling gurus. Unlike smaller mushrooms, it's easy to handle over the flames, and it makes a meaty, satisfying addition to this Mediterranean-inspired sandwich.

DIRECT/MEDIUM HEAT

- 4 **fresh portobello mushrooms, about 3 ounces each**
- 2 **red or yellow bell peppers, 6 to 8 ounces each**
- 2 **yellow squashes, about 6 ounces each, ends trimmed**
- 1 **large ripe tomato, about 8 ounces**
- ½ **cup olive oil**
- 1 **tablespoon chopped fresh rosemary**
- 1 **tablespoon finely chopped shallot**
- ½ **teaspoon kosher salt**
- ¼ **teaspoon freshly ground pepper**
- 3 **tablespoons balsamic vinegar**
- 8 **slices soft-crusted French or Italian bread, each ½ inch thick, or soft rolls**
- 8 **ounces fresh goat cheese**
- 12 to 16 **fresh basil leaves**

REMOVE THE STEMS from the mushrooms. Cut the bell peppers in half lengthwise. Remove the seeds and flatten the peppers with the palm of your hand. Cut the squashes lengthwise into ½-inch-thick slices. Cut the tomato crosswise into ½-inch-thick slices. Put the vegetables in a lock-top plastic bag large enough to hold them.

In a small bowl, whisk together the olive oil, rosemary, shallot, salt, and pepper. Add this mixture to the bag of vegetables. Allow the vegetables to marinate at room temperature for 10 to 15 minutes.

Remove the vegetables from the bag. Grill them directly over medium heat, turning once, until tender. The mushrooms will take 12 to 14 minutes, the bell peppers 10 to 12 minutes, the squashes 8 to 10 minutes, and the tomato 3 to 4 minutes. Transfer to a large platter. Drizzle the grilled vegetables with the balsamic vinegar. Season with salt and pepper to taste.

Evenly spread the goat cheese onto one side of a bread slice. Build the sandwiches with the grilled vegetables, interspersing the basil leaves as you build. Place the remaining bread slices on top.

Serve warm or at room temperature.

MAKES 4 SERVINGS

WINE NOTES: *A fresh Dolcetto or young Zinfandel with fruit to burn, but not much in the way of oak or tannin to complicate matters, would be ideal here.*

Mixed Vegetable Grill
with Roasted Garlic Marinade

The many virtues associated with grilled vegetables certainly include good health and dynamic flavors. Here, a subtly sweet roasted garlic vinaigrette is used as a marinade. With a little planning, you can add the vegetables to the grill according to thickness and tenderness, so all of them finish at the same time.

DIRECT/MEDIUM HEAT

- 2 **heads garlic**
- 2 **tablespoons plus 1 cup extra-virgin olive oil**
- ¼ **cup balsamic vinegar**
- 2 **tablespoons red wine vinegar**
- 2 **teaspoons kosher salt**
- 1 **teaspoon freshly ground pepper**
- 3 **red or yellow bell peppers, 7 to 8 ounces each**
- 6 **pattypan squashes, about 2 ounces each**
- 1 **Japanese eggplant, 4 to 5 ounces**
- 1 **green or yellow zucchini, 5 to 6 ounces**
- 10 **asparagus spears, about 8 ounces total**
- 1 **ear of corn, husked, 7 to 8 ounces**
- 1 **head Belgian endive, about 4 ounces**
- 4 **fresh shiitake mushrooms, about 1 ounce each**
- 1 **baby bok choy, 6 to 7 ounces**
- 2 **plum tomatoes, 1 to 2 ounces each**

REMOVE AS MUCH of the outer papery skin as possible from the garlic heads. Using a sharp knife, slice off the top quarter of the heads to expose the pulp. Drizzle 1 tablespoon of the olive oil over each head, then wrap each separately in aluminum foil. Place on the cooking grate directly over medium heat and cook until the pulp is golden brown and tender, 35 to 40 minutes. Remove from the cooking grate and allow to cool. (The garlic can be grilled up to a day in advance.) Unwrap the bulbs and carefully squeeze the pulp into a food processor or blender, discarding the skins. Add the remaining 1 cup olive oil, the balsamic vinegar, red wine vinegar, salt, and pepper. Process until smooth. Transfer the marinade to a bowl (or lock-top plastic bag) large enough to hold the vegetables.

Cut the bell peppers in half lengthwise. Remove the stems, core, and seeds and flatten the peppers with the palm of your hand. Trim the stem ends from the pattypan squashes, eggplant, zucchini, and asparagus. Cut the ear of corn in half crosswise. Cut the Belgian endive in half lengthwise. Trim the tough stems from the shiitake mushrooms. Cut the baby bok choy in half lengthwise. Core the plum tomatoes. Place all of the vegetables in the bowl (or bag) with the marinade. Toss to coat thoroughly. Allow to marinate in the refrigerator for at least 1 hour or as long as 4 hours.

Grill the vegetables directly over medium heat according to the directions and times indicated on page 205. Serve warm.

MAKES 6 SERVINGS

WINE NOTES: *The Rhône-style white varietals Marsanne, Roussanne, and Viognier all pair well with roasted vegetables.*

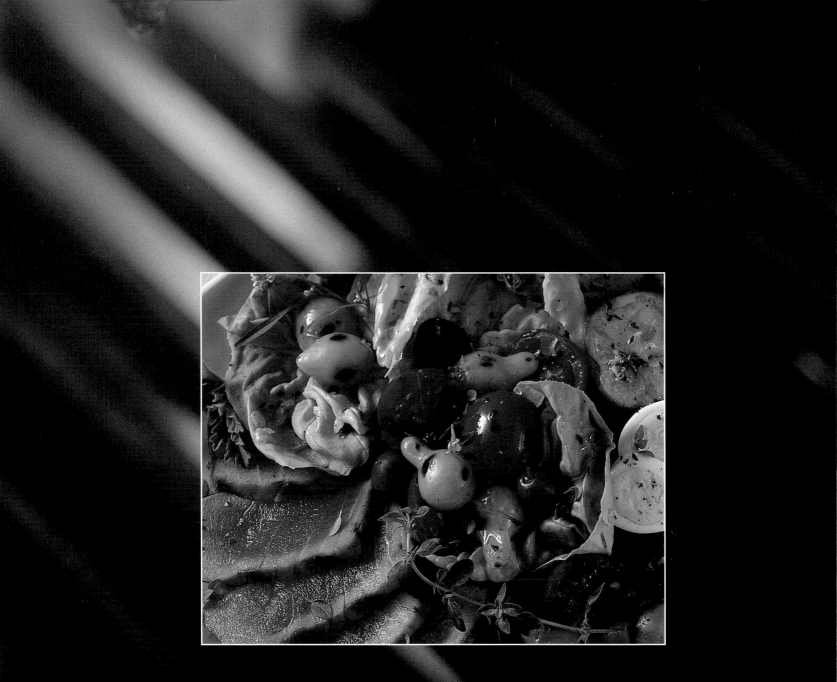

Even though the main course often fills the most space on our plates, the foods served on the side go a long way to define the spirit of a meal. Like music or table settings, they can point the dining experience in a particular regional direction or express the level of formality. For instance, while a warm bowl of baked beans or wedge of cornbread suggest a laid-back American barbecue, Tuscan-style artichokes or tuna Niçoise contribute to a European sense of place.

When you serve just the right side or salad, you ground the main dish in familiar flavor combinations that guests appreciate, such as hand-cut French fries or garlic-roasted potatoes with a juicy, sizzling steak. Give these recipes their due attention and they will brilliantly perform supporting roles.

Several side dishes can be made well ahead of whatever main item you are cooking, and kept warm or left at room temperature. When you are focusing on a prime rib or planked salmon, and waiting for that point of perfect doneness, it helps to have a brilliant side or salad ready in the wings.

sides & salads

Tuscan-Style Artichokes

Tuscans relish outdoor grilling, particularly in the spring when the weather is kind and globe artichokes abound. Braising them first in olive oil, wine, and herbs ensures that they are tender and flavorful. Just prior to serving, turn them on the grill for a few minutes to add an unmistakably rustic quality.

DIRECT/HIGH HEAT

3 medium artichokes,
    8 to 10 ounces each

    Juice of 1 lemon

½ cup olive oil

3 tablespoons white wine vinegar

¼ cup dry white wine

3 large cloves garlic, thinly sliced

1 tablespoon chopped fresh parsley

1 tablespoon chopped fresh thyme

½ teaspoon kosher salt

¼ teaspoon freshly ground pepper

PREHEAT THE OVEN to 450°F.

Cut each artichoke into quarters lengthwise, dropping them immediately into a bowl of water with the juice of 1 lemon, to avoid discoloring. With a small, sharp knife, scoop out and discard the hairy choke.

In a large sauté pan, mix the olive oil, vinegar, wine, garlic, parsley, thyme, salt, and pepper. Arrange the artichoke quarters in one layer, with one cut side facing down, in the sauté pan. Place the pan on the stovetop or side burner, and bring the mixture to boil over high heat for about 30 seconds. Then place the pan in the oven and roast the artichokes, turning once so that the other cut sides face down, until golden brown and barely tender, about 15 minutes total. The artichoke quarters may be prepared to this point several hours ahead and set aside at room temperature.

Pick up the artichoke quarters (with tongs, if hot) and allow any excess oil to drip away. Grill the artichokes directly over high heat, turning occasionally, until they are nicely browned, 4 to 5 minutes. Serve warm.

MAKES 4 SERVINGS

Hand-Cut French Fries
with Spicy Ketchup

Glorious French fries are only minutes away with a hot grill and some basic pantry ingredients. Roasted to a golden brown, then dunked into a deliciously doctored ketchup, they won't last more than a few minutes. And no one will need to worry about all the fat and calories present in deep-fried versions.

DIRECT/MEDIUM HEAT

¼ cup ketchup

½ teaspoon chile sauce

½ teaspoon balsamic vinegar

2 russet potatoes, about
   8 ounces each

1 tablespoon olive oil

1 tablespoon minced garlic

½ teaspoon kosher salt

½ teaspoon freshly ground pepper

IN A SMALL BOWL, mix together the ketchup, chile sauce, and balsamic vinegar. Set aside.

Scrub the potatoes under cold running water and dry thoroughly, but do not peel. Cut lengthwise into ½-inch-thick slices, then cut the slices into ¼-inch-thick wedges. Place the wedges in a medium bowl. Toss with the olive oil, garlic, salt, and pepper.

Place the wedges on the grill, being careful not to let them drop through the openings. Cook directly over medium heat until golden brown, turning once, about 10 minutes. For extra-crispy fries, open the grill and cook for an additional 1 to 2 minutes, turning once.

Serve warm with the ketchup.

MAKES 4 SERVINGS

Garlic-Roasted Potatoes on Rosemary Skewers

Skewers fashioned from sturdy rosemary branches add a subtle flavor to this simple dish, and make for a notable presentation. Balsamic vinegar and olive oil lend an appealing bite. If rosemary is unavailable, bamboo skewers can be substituted. Soak them in water for at least 30 minutes beforehand.

DIRECT/MEDIUM HEAT

1 **pound red or white new potatoes, each about 1½ inches in diameter**

   About ½ cup extra-virgin olive oil

1 **tablespoon minced garlic**

   Kosher salt

   Freshly ground pepper

6 **sturdy rosemary branches**

⅓ **cup balsamic vinegar**

CUT THE POTATOES IN HALF, and place in a medium bowl. Add 2 tablespoons of olive oil and the garlic. Season with salt and pepper to taste.

Strip almost all of the leaves from the rosemary branches to form skewers, leaving some leaves near the slightly thinner end. Finely chop enough leaves to measure 2 tablespoons and add them to the potatoes. Toss the potatoes to coat thoroughly with the oil and seasonings. Using the thicker end of each rosemary skewer as a point, thread the potato halves onto the skewers, dividing them evenly.

Grill the skewers directly over medium heat until the skins begin to brown and crisp, 25 to 30 minutes.

Pour the balsamic vinegar into a small sauté pan over high heat and boil until reduced to about 2 tablespoons, about 4 minutes (the vinegar will be syrupy). Pour enough of the remaining olive oil onto a serving platter to form a thin layer. Sprinkle the oil with salt and pepper to taste. Drizzle the warm vinegar over the oil. Place the skewers on the platter, turn the potatoes in the oil and vinegar, and serve immediately.

MAKES 4 TO 6 SERVINGS

Acorn Squash with Spiced Pecan Butter

On cool autumn nights, a sweet, buttery glaze over tender acorn squash is about as comforting as food gets. If you like, substitute butternut squash for equally good results. Either makes a worthy companion to baked ham and mashed potatoes or a Thanksgiving turkey.

INDIRECT/HIGH HEAT

FOR THE BUTTER:

¼ cup unsalted butter,
   at room temperature

⅓ cup chopped toasted pecans

1 tablespoon maple syrup

½ teaspoon ground cinnamon

½ teaspoon kosher salt

¼ teaspoon ground ginger

¼ teaspoon freshly ground pepper

FOR THE SQUASH:

2 acorn squashes, 1½ to
   2 pounds each

2 teaspoons olive oil

Kosher salt

Freshly ground pepper

TO MAKE THE BUTTER: In a small bowl, combine the butter, pecans, maple syrup, cinnamon, salt, ginger, and pepper. Mix well with a fork.

With a large, heavy knife, cut the squash in half lengthwise. Remove the seeds with a spoon. Lightly brush the exposed flesh with the olive oil. Season with salt and pepper to taste.

Put the squash halves, cut sides down, on the cooking grate and grill indirectly over high heat until grill marks are clearly visible, about 30 minutes. Turn the squash halves cut sides up. Spread the exposed flesh with the pecan butter. Continue grilling indirectly over high heat until the flesh is tender, 20 to 30 minutes. Serve warm.

MAKES 4 SERVINGS

Bourbon Barbecue Beans

You can make beans like these from scratch, but the truth is most of the best barbecue joints in the Midwest start with canned pork and beans. If you happen to have any leftover bits of barbecue beef or pork, toss them in. And don't forget a douse of bourbon to bring the flavors to life.

INDIRECT/MEDIUM HEAT

4 **slices bacon (about 3 ounces), cut into ½-inch dice**

1 **cup diced yellow onions (½-inch dice)**

1 **tablespoon minced garlic**

½ **cup ketchup**

¼ **cup dark molasses**

¼ **cup yellow mustard**

¼ **cup bourbon**

2 **tablespoons brown sugar**

2 **tablespoons Worcestershire sauce**

3 or 4 **dashes Tabasco sauce**

2 **cans (28 ounces each) baked beans**

Kosher salt

Freshly ground pepper

Mesquite or hickory chips, soaked in water for at least 30 minutes

IN A LARGE SAUTÉ PAN over medium heat, cook the bacon, stirring occasionally, until crispy, about 10 minutes. Add the onions and garlic and cook, until soft, about 5 minutes. Add the ketchup, molasses, mustard, bourbon, brown sugar, Worcestershire sauce, and Tabasco sauce. Bring to a boil, reduce the heat, and simmer for about 5 minutes.

Follow the grill's instructions for using wood chips, and set up the grill for indirect cooking.

Rinse and drain the baked beans and put them in a 2-quart casserole or Dutch oven. Add the sauce from the sauté pan. Stir to combine thoroughly. Place the pan on the cooking grate over indirect medium heat. Cook for 1½ to 2 hours. Season with salt and pepper to taste. Serve warm.

MAKES 12 TO 15 SERVINGS

Sides & Salads

Cast-Iron Skillet Cornbread

Cornbread draws appreciation at just about every barbecue. With corn kernels, fiery jalapeños, and roasted red bell peppers in the batter, a good idea gets even better.

INDIRECT/MEDIUM HEAT

- 2 **ears of corn in husks, silks trimmed**
- 2 **cups yellow cornmeal**
- 1½ **cups plus 2 tablespoons all-purpose flour**
- ½ **cup sugar**
- 1 **tablespoon baking powder**
- 2 **teaspoons baking soda**
- 2 **teaspoons kosher salt**
- 3 **eggs**
- 1 **cup milk**
- 1 **jalapeño chile, minced, including seeds**
- 1 **roasted red bell pepper, finely diced**
- ½ **cup unsalted butter**
- 1 **cup sour cream**

PLACE THE CORN in a deep container, cover with cold water and soak for at least 1 hour. Remove the corn from the container; shake to remove excess water. Grill the corn indirectly over medium heat, 25 to 30 minutes, turning several times. Let cool, then remove husks and silk.

In a large bowl, combine the cornmeal, flour, sugar, baking powder, baking soda, and salt. Mix well, breaking up any lumps with a whisk. In a medium bowl, whisk together the eggs, milk, chile, bell pepper, and corn kernels. Add the wet mixture to the dry mixture and stir with a wooden spoon until just blended.

In a 10-inch cast-iron skillet over medium heat, melt the butter. Pour the butter into the cornmeal mixture and stir with the wooden spoon until just blended.

Pour the batter into the unwiped hot skillet, spreading it evenly in the pan. If any butter collects around the edges of the skillet, spoon it over the top of the batter. Place the skillet on the cooking grate over indirect medium heat. Cook until the cornbread is golden brown around the edges and a toothpick inserted in the center comes out clean, 25 to 30 minutes. Allow to cool to room temperature in the skillet.

Invert the cornbread onto a plate or cutting board. Cut into wedges and serve with sour cream.

MAKES 8 SERVINGS

SETTINGS:
business casual

A "business casual" event doesn't have to be a contradiction in terms. It can be as simple as inviting colleagues or clients to a dinner at your home. This creates a rare opportunity for everyone to truly relax and to enjoy the pleasures of home-cooked food. And it doesn't have to be difficult. With early planning and careful execution, you'll find this meal surprisingly easy, and your guests will enjoy it more than any other corporate occasion.

First step: Think about potential guests. Choose people with similar rank, common interests, and complementary personalities. As for numbers, it's usually better to invite fewer guests rather than more, so

you won't stretch yourself too thin. Once you've decided whom to invite, choose the time of day. In summertime, you might serve a twilight dinner, preceded by drinks and a friendly game of croquet. A tray of cocktails helps to loosen the collars—or you might even serve fresh lemonade.

Before your guests arrive, have the table all set. A round table works well, because everyone can hear everything, and every seat is equal. (However, if you wish to observe old-school etiquette, try placing the highest-ranking guest to your right and the second-highest-ranking guest to your left. Everyone else may be seated at random.) Set out a tablecloth and napkins in matching or complementary colors, with plates stacked for easy serving of successive courses. For the centerpiece, choose flowers that echo the colors of the plates. Individual bud vases at each place add a graceful note; if you

the art of the mix

wish, place cards make seating quick and easy.

For the food, begin with a starter, soup, or salad, followed by the main course. Consider setting out "one-handed" appetizers—such as skewered shrimp, chicken wings, or bruschetta—that can be enjoyed while walking around and conversing (or swinging a croquet mallet). But this is probably not the evening to experiment. Try choosing dishes that are both simple and

sophisticated, and recipes that you've tested and enjoyed at least once beforehand. You want to be able to juggle both the grilling and the guests with equal grace. Grilled lobster tails are an excellent choice. Their rich, succulent flavor satisfies everyone from fish fanatics to meat lovers—and they're simple to cook. Alongside, consider grilled corn on the cob, a mixed vegetable grill, or for a more sophisticated touch, garlic-roasted potatoes on rosemary skewers.

For the wine, you might try a lobster-friendly French Burgundy such as Gevrey-Chambertin or Puligny-Montrachet, or a Chardonnay or Viognier from California.

Once the dinner plates are cleared away, serve something fresh and light, such as strawberries with port or with a syrup made of balsamic vinegar and sugar. On the other hand, few guests will refuse the whimsical yet classy version of "s'mores" presented in this book.

Chicken and Mesclun Salad with Raspberry-Walnut Vinaigrette

An off-the-beaten-path vinaigrette based on walnut oil and raspberry vinegar will have guests wondering what the secret of this delicious salad is. For easy seasonal variations, substitute grilled prawns, scallops, or sliced pork tenderloin for the chicken.

INDIRECT/MEDIUM HEAT

FOR THE VINAIGRETTE:

½ cup walnut oil

3 tablespoons raspberry vinegar

1 tablespoon maple syrup

½ teaspoon kosher salt

¼ teaspoon freshly ground pepper

FOR THE SALAD:

2 tablespoons olive oil

Juice of 1 lemon

½ teaspoon kosher salt

¼ teaspoon freshly ground pepper

3 boneless chicken breasts, 7 to 8 ounces each

6 ounces mesclun (mixed young greens)

¾ cup coarsely chopped toasted pecans

½ pint (1 cup) raspberries

TO MAKE THE VINAIGRETTE: In a small bowl, whisk together the walnut oil, raspberry vinegar, maple syrup, salt, and pepper.

In a medium bowl, whisk together the olive oil, lemon juice, salt, and pepper. Add the chicken breasts and turn them to coat thoroughly. Place the chicken breasts, skin side down, over indirect medium heat, and grill, turning once, until the juices run clear, 10 to 12 minutes total. Remove the chicken breasts from the grill and cut them into ¼-inch-thick slices.

Place the mesclun in a large bowl and toss with about three-quarters of the vinaigrette. Divide the mesclun evenly among individual plates. Arrange the chicken slices over the greens. Garnish each plate with the pecans and raspberries. Drizzle the remaining vinaigrette over the top. Serve at room temperature.

MAKES 4 SERVINGS

Grilled Tuna Niçoise

This traditional salad from southern France, which typically calls for well-done tuna, rises to new heights with sushi-grade tuna grilled rare to medium-rare. You can cook the ingredients several hours before you plan to serve this salad and lay them out on plates at the last minute. It's a captivating opening course or, in slightly larger portions, a meal in itself.

DIRECT/MEDIUM HEAT

FOR THE VINAIGRETTE:

¾ **cup extra-virgin olive oil**

¼ **cup sherry vinegar**

2 **tablespoons minced shallot**

1½ **tablespoons finely chopped fresh oregano**

Kosher salt

Freshly ground pepper

FOR THE SALAD:

4 **eggs**

6 **small red new potatoes, about 10 ounces total**

Salt

10 **ounces haricots verts (thin green beans), stem ends trimmed**

4 **sushi-grade tuna steaks, each 6 to 7 ounces, 1 inch thick**

1 **small head butter lettuce (about 4 ounces), leaves separated**

12 **Niçoise olives**

10 **to 15 small pear tomatoes, halved lengthwise, or 3 plum tomatoes, cut into ¼-inch-thick slices**

TO MAKE THE VINAIGRETTE: In a small bowl, whisk together the oil, vinegar, shallot, and oregano. Season with salt and pepper to taste.

Bring a large saucepan filled three-quarters with water to a simmer. Lower the eggs into the water and allow to simmer until hard-boiled, 8 to 10 minutes. With a slotted spoon, remove the eggs and cool them under cold running water. Tap the eggs all over to crack the shells, then peel them and cut lengthwise into quarters. Return the water in the saucepan to a boil, add the potatoes, and boil until barely tender, about 10 minutes. Remove the potatoes with a slotted spoon and, when cool enough to handle, cut them in half. Return the water to a boil, add a teaspoon or two of salt, then add the green beans. Boil until barely tender, 2 to 3 minutes. Drain and cool under cold running water.

Place the tuna and the potatoes in a shallow dish. Pour ¼ cup of the vinaigrette over them. Turn to coat well.

Grill the potatoes directly over medium heat, turning once, until golden brown, 8 to 10 minutes total. Grill the tuna directly over medium heat, turning once, for 4 to 5 minutes total for rare (8 to 10 minutes total for well done). Cut the tuna across the grain into ¼-inch-thick slices.

Arrange a couple of butter lettuce leaves on each plate with some olives and tomatoes. Place the eggs, beans, and potatoes around the plate. Fan the tuna slices across the lettuce. Drizzle the remaining vinaigrette over the salad. Serve at room temperature.

MAKES 4 SERVINGS

desserts

Simple, familiar desserts are usually the most welcome finishes to traditional barbecues. People like to bask a little longer in the informal feeling of the meal and let something soothing like a berry crisp or creamy cheesecake carry their taste buds gently to the meal's conclusion. Made-ahead desserts, like a strawberry mousse or chocolate tartlets, free the cook from doing anything but setting them down before appreciative guests.

Nevertheless, there are grillers who relish the opportunity to close an elaborate dinner with one more testimony to the grill's ability to coax flavor from nearly all foods, including fruit. Witness a dish of grilled peaches or a banana-and-mango napoleon. For the best results, clean the cooking grate thoroughly. Use melted butter or a neutral-flavored vegetable oil as a baste. And cook sweet, tender fruits only a few minutes—just long enough to lightly caramelize their natural sugars.

S'Mores All Grown Up

Some childhood icons, such as the original version of this campfire dessert, are so inspired that they qualify for adult status, too. Embellished with premium chocolate and candied orange zest, these treats have the power to persuade all of us that one is good, but s'more is better.

DIRECT/HIGH HEAT

Peel of 1 medium orange, with most of the white pith removed, cut into ¼-inch-wide strips

2 **cups plus 2 tablespoons sugar**

8 **graham crackers, each one split in half**

8 **thin squares (2 inches each) premium chocolate such as Valhrona**

8 **large marshmallows**

4 **long metal skewers (or 4 long bamboo skewers soaked in water for at least 30 minutes)**

BRING A SMALL SAUCEPAN filled three-quarters with water to a boil. Add the orange strips, blanch for 2 minutes, and then drain. In the same small saucepan, bring 2 cups water and the 2 cups sugar to a boil, stirring to dissolve the sugar. Reduce the heat to a simmer, add the orange strips, and simmer, stirring occasionally, until tender, about 10 minutes. Have a small bowl ready with the remaining 2 tablespoons of sugar in it. Drain the orange strips and quickly put them in the bowl of sugar, tossing them with a fork or tongs. Allow the orange strips to dry on a rack at room temperature for 24 hours.

Place each graham cracker half on a plate, setting a square of chocolate on top of each one. Add 1 or 2 pieces of candied orange peel to each piece of chocolate. Thread 2 marshmallows onto the end of each skewer. Hold the marshmallows just above the cooking grate directly over high heat and turn slowly until lightly browned, 2 to 3 minutes.

Slide a warm marshmallow onto each square, placing the remaining graham cracker halves on top. Gently press together and wait until the marshmallows melt the chocolate slightly, about 1 minute. Serve immediately.

MAKES 8 S'MORES

Grilled Peaches with Fresh Cherry Sauce

In the late 1800s, famous French chef Auguste Escoffier created a dessert for Dame Nellie Melba, a celebrated Australian opera singer. Called peach Melba, the immediately popular recipe consisted of poached peaches, vanilla ice cream, and raspberry sauce. Here is a twist on that classic summertime dish.

DIRECT/MEDIUM HEAT

FOR THE SAUCE:

- 1 **pound dark cherries, pitted (about 1 cup)**
- 1 **tablespoon sugar**
- ½ **cup dry red wine**
- 1 **teaspoon balsamic vinegar**
- 1 **teaspoon kirsch (cherry liqueur)**

FOR THE PEACHES:

- 4 **medium peaches**
- 2 **tablespoons unsalted butter**
- 2 **tablespoons brown sugar**
- 1 **cup vanilla ice cream**
- 4 **cookies**

TO MAKE THE CHERRY SAUCE: In a sauté pan over medium-high heat, combine the pitted cherries, sugar, red wine, and balsamic vinegar. Bring to a simmer and cook, stirring occasionally, until the fruit is soft, 6 to 8 minutes. Transfer the mixture to a food processor and puree until completely smooth. Return the mixture to the sauté pan over medium-high heat. Add the kirsch. Simmer until reduced to about ¼ cup, 1 to 2 minutes.

Cut the peaches in half and remove and discard the pits. Place the halves in a medium bowl. In a small saucepan set over low heat, melt the butter and brown sugar together. Coat the peaches with the butter mixture. Grill the peaches directly over medium heat, turning once, until grill marks are clearly visible and the peaches are soft, 10 to 12 minutes total.

While the peaches are still warm, layer each serving glass with 2 peach halves, 1 scoop ice cream, and 1 tablespoon cherry sauce. Tuck a cookie into each glass. Serve immediately.

MAKES 4 SERVINGS

Silky Cheesecake with Summer Fruit

Mixing the filling of this voluptuous cheesecake for a full twenty minutes guarantees an utterly smooth and airy center that almost dissolves on your tongue. It's best to make this dessert the day before a big barbecue. Tucked away in the refrigerator, it stands ready to seal the meal with style.

1¾ cups (about 9 ounces) graham cracker crumbs

¼ cup unsalted butter, melted

1 tablespoon brown sugar

1½ pounds cream cheese, at room temperature

4 eggs

1¾ cups granulated sugar

1 teaspoon vanilla extract

2 cups (1 pint) sour cream

2 ripe peaches

½ pint fresh raspberries

IN A MEDIUM BOWL, stir together the graham cracker crumbs, butter, and brown sugar, mixing well. Press the mixture into an even layer on the bottom of a 9-inch springform pan.

Preheat the oven to 325°F.

Using a stand mixer fitted with a flat beater attachment, beat together the cream cheese, eggs, 1 cup of the granulated sugar, and the vanilla at medium speed until very smooth, about 20 minutes. Pour into the crust-lined springform pan.

Bake until the cake has puffed over the rim of the pan and the top is slightly cracked around the edges, 1 to 1¼ hours. Transfer the pan to a rack, cover, and allow to cool for 30 minutes. (As the cake cools, it will sink back below the rim of the pan.) Leave the oven set at 325°F.

In a small bowl, mix together the sour cream and the remaining ¾ cup granulated sugar. Pour this mixture over the top of the cake, and return the cake to the oven for 10 minutes. Remove from the oven, allow to cool to room temperature, cover, and refrigerate for at least 8 hours or as long as 2 days.

Remove the sides of the pan and slide the cake onto a serving plate. Cut the peaches in half and remove the pits. Thinly slice the peaches and overlap the slices around the top edge of the cheesecake. Pile the raspberries in the center.

To serve, slice the cake with a clean knife dipped in hot water before each cut, being sure to cut all the way through the crust.

MAKES 10 TO 12 SERVINGS

Berry Biscotti Crisp

Cobblers, grunts, and pandowdies are all deep-dish fruit desserts that call for some form of pastry dough on top. A crisp is an even easier way to go because all you do is scatter a sweet crumbly mixture over the fruit. The flavors and textures of biscotti crumbs and toasted almonds marry perfectly with bubbling blueberries and raspberries. Vanilla ice cream makes an excellent accompaniment.

INDIRECT/HIGH HEAT

1½ **pints (3 cups) fresh blueberries**

1 **pint (2 cups) fresh raspberries**

3 **tablespoons brown sugar**

FOR THE TOPPING:

¼ **cup all-purpose flour**

2½ **tablespoons brown sugar**

¼ **teaspoon ground cinnamon**

¼ **teaspoon kosher salt**

2 **tablespoons unsalted butter, cut into ½-inch pieces**

¼ **cup (about 1 ounce) finely ground almond biscotti**

¼ **cup roughly chopped toasted almonds**

IN A MEDIUM BOWL, gently mix together the blueberries, raspberries, and brown sugar. Spoon the mixture into a 9-inch pie pan.

To make the topping: In a medium bowl, stir together the flour, brown sugar, cinnamon, and salt. Add the butter. Using your fingertips, break the butter into smaller pieces, coating them with the dry ingredients. Add the ground biscotti and toasted almonds. Stir to combine. Sprinkle over the fruit.

Cook the crisp indirectly over high heat until bubbling and lightly browned along the edges, 20 to 25 minutes. Allow to cool for 5 minutes. Spoon into serving dishes while still warm.

MAKES 8 SERVINGS

Chocolate Cointreau Tartlets

In this recipe, two shades of ganache, the cream and chocolate mixture that is the essence of all sweet truffles, are poured into a small pastry shell and swirled together to create an appealing design. Flavor the ganache with any liqueur or extract you like for an authentic truffle taste.

FOR THE DOUGH:

1½ cups all-purpose flour

2 tablespoons sugar

¼ teaspoon salt

½ cup chilled unsalted butter, cut into 8 pieces

1 egg yolk mixed with ¼ cup ice water

FOR THE FILLING:

6 ounces semisweet chocolate, finely chopped

6 ounces milk chocolate, finely chopped

½ cup heavy cream

¼ cup Cointreau (orange liqueur)

FOR GARNISH (OPTIONAL):

½ pint (1 cup) raspberries

8 fresh mint sprigs

TO MAKE THE DOUGH: In a large bowl, stir together the flour, sugar, and salt. Using a pastry blender, cut in the butter until the mixture has the consistency of coarse meal. Add the egg yolk mixture and stir with a fork until the dough begins to hold together. (If it seems too dry, stir in another teaspoon of ice water.) Gather the dough into a ball, flatten into a disk, wrap, and refrigerate for at least 30 minutes.

On a lightly floured surface, roll out the dough into a rectangle about ⅛ inch thick. Cut out 8 rounds, each large enough to line a 3-inch fluted tartlet pan. Line the pans with the rounds and trim the edges even with the rim. Refrigerate for 30 minutes.

Preheat the oven to 375°F.

Prick the bottom of each crust several times with a fork. Line with a piece of aluminum foil and fill with pie weights or uncooked rice. Bake until the edges begin to brown, about 20 minutes. Remove the weights and foil and return the pans to the oven. Bake until light brown and fully cooked, 15 to 18 minutes. Allow to cool on a rack.

To make the filling: Place the semisweet chocolate in a medium bowl. Place the milk chocolate in another medium bowl. In a saucepan, bring the cream and Cointreau to a boil. Add half of the cream mixture to the semisweet chocolate and half to the milk chocolate. Quickly stir each mixture until smooth.

With a spoon in each hand, pour some of each chocolate simultaneously down opposite sides of one of the crusts so the chocolates touch near the middle, dividing the filling into two colors. Repeat with the remaining chocolate and crusts. Using the tip of a thin knife, pull some of each chocolate to the opposite side of each tartlet, creating a design. Cover and refrigerate the tartlets for at least 1 hour or as long as 24 hours.

Serve at room temperature with raspberries and mint sprigs, if desired.

MAKES 8 THREE-INCH TARTLETS

Banana and Mango Napoleon

This dazzling finale actually comes together much more easily than it appears. With puff pastry purchased from the store, there's little left to do except make the luscious pastry cream and grill the fruit. Everything can be cooked ahead of time and assembled in layers when you're ready to serve.

DIRECT/LOW HEAT

FOR THE PASTRY CREAM:

3 egg yolks

Pinch of kosher salt

⅓ cup granulated sugar

2 tablespoons all-purpose flour

1 cup milk

1 tablespoon dark rum

½ vanilla bean, split lengthwise

1 tablespoon unsalted butter

**¼ cup heavy cream, whipped
into soft peaks**

FOR THE FILLING:

**1 sheet frozen puff pastry, about
9 inches square, thawed**

1 tablespoon brown sugar

2 tablespoons unsalted butter

Juice of 1 lime

**3 firm, ripe bananas, about 5 ounces
each, peeled, halved crosswise, and
then halved lengthwise**

**1 firm, ripe mango, about 6 ounces,
peeled, pitted, and cut into twelve
½-inch-thick slices**

2 tablespoons confectioners' sugar

½ teaspoon ground cinnamon

TO MAKE THE PASTRY CREAM: In a small bowl, whisk together the egg yolks, salt, and half of the granulated sugar until the sugar dissolves. Whisk in the flour. In a small saucepan, combine the milk, rum, and the remaining granulated sugar. With the tip of a knife, scrape the vanilla seeds into the pan. Bring the mixture to a boil over high heat. Slowly pour half of the hot mixture into the egg mixture, whisking constantly. Reduce the heat to medium. Pour the egg mixture back into the saucepan, whisking constantly. Continue whisking until the pastry cream comes to a boil and thickens, 1 to 2 minutes. Remove from the heat, whisk in the butter, and pour into a bowl. Press plastic wrap directly onto the surface to prevent a skin from forming. Refrigerate until needed. When ready to use, whisk in the whipped cream.

Preheat the oven to 350°F.

Cut the pastry sheet into nine 3-inch squares. With a fork, prick each square about 15 times to prevent the dough from rising too much in the oven. Place on a baking sheet. Bake until golden brown, 20 to 25 minutes. Carefully slice each square horizontally into two layers.

In a small saucepan over medium heat, melt together the brown sugar, butter, and lime juice, stirring occasionally. Pour into a medium bowl, add the bananas and mangoes, and toss to coat. Grill the bananas and mangoes directly over low heat, without turning, until grill marks are clearly visible, about 2 minutes.

To make each napoleon, place a layer of pastry on each plate. Spoon some pastry cream on top. Place a piece of banana and a piece of mango on the pastry cream. Top with another layer of pastry. Spoon on more pastry cream, then top with more banana and mango. Finally, place a third pastry layer on top. Put the confectioners' sugar and cinnamon in a fine-meshed sieve and, lightly tapping on the side, dust the napoleons. Serve at room temperature.

MAKES 6 SERVINGS

Strawberry Mousse

Sometimes a magnificently grilled main course is best followed by an utterly simple dessert. A judicious amount of gelatin supports the airy texture of this refreshing mousse. It looks particularly good served in swanky stemware, such as martini glasses. You can make this dessert the day before the party and still bring it to the table with pizazz.

---

2 pints (4 cups) strawberries, hulled

⅓ cup sugar

1 tablespoon fresh lemon juice

¼ teaspoon vanilla extract

1 envelope (2¼ teaspoons) gelatin

1 cup heavy cream

IN A MEDIUM SAUCEPAN over high heat, combine 1½ pints of the strawberries (reserve the rest for garnish), the sugar, lemon juice, and vanilla. Bring to a boil and cook until the strawberries are soft, about 5 minutes. Transfer to a food processor or blender and puree until smooth. Pour into a small saucepan over low heat and keep warm.

Pour ¼ cup cold water into a small bowl. Add the gelatin and let soften for 5 minutes. Transfer the gelatin mixture to the warm strawberry purée and stir until the gelatin melts. Remove from the heat and allow to return to room temperature.

In a large bowl, whip the cream until it holds stiff peaks. Add the strawberry purée and fold the ingredients together. Pour into serving containers. Cover and refrigerate for at least 4 hours or as long as 2 days.

Serve cold, garnished with sliced strawberries.

MAKES 4 SERVINGS

Appendix

Cooking Tips and Helpful Hints

- Always preheat the grill before cooking. Set all burners on high and close the lid; heat for 10 minutes, or until the thermometer reads 500-550°F.

- Always cook with the lid down for best results.

- Grilling times in charts and recipes are approximate. Times can vary depending on weather, or the amount, size, and shape of the food to be cooked. Allow more cooking time on cold or windy days or at higher altitudes and less cooking time in extremely hot weather.

- Foods on a crowded cooking grate will require more cooking time than just a few foods. Foods cooked in containers, such as baked beans, will require more time if cooked in a deep casserole rather than a shallow baking pan.

- Trim excess fat from steaks, chops, and roasts, leaving no more than a scant ¼-inch-thick layer. Less fat guards against unwanted flare-ups and makes cleanup easier.

- When using a marinade, sauce, or glaze with a high sugar content, or other ingredients that burn easily, brush it on food only during the last 10 to 15 minutes of grilling.

- Use an instant-read thermometer to check for doneness in roasts, chickens, turkeys, or other thick cuts of meat. Never leave a thermometer in the food while grilling.

- When handling meats, use tongs rather than a fork to avoid losing natural juices. Use two spatulas for handling large whole fish. Avoid flattening burgers with a spatula; when pressed, flavorful juices escape, leaving burgers dry.

- If an unwanted flare-up should occur, turn all burners to OFF and move food to another area of the cooking grate. Any flames will quickly subside. After flames subside, re-light the grill. Never use water to extinguish flames on a gas barbecue.

- Some foods, such as casseroles or thin fish fillets, require a container for grilling. Disposable aluminum pans are convenient, but any metal pan with ovenproof handles can be used.

- If your grill has a grease catch pan, be sure to keep it clean and free from debris.

- Using a timer will help alert you when "well-done" is about to become "over-done."

- To keep foods from sticking, brush a light coating of cooking oil on the cooking grate just before placing foods on it.

Tips for Cooking Entire Meals on the Grill

- Incorporate some dishes that can be partially or completely made ahead.

- Select recipes that use produce that is in season and at peak ripeness.

- Compose the menu from dishes that provide complementary flavors, colors, and textures.

- Look for recipes that can be cooked simultaneously, or comfortably in sequence. A dessert that will be served warm can be made first and should be just right for eating after the main meal has been served. Or an appetizer or two can be cooked first and served to guests with drinks while the entrée and side dishes are cooking.

- For dishes that will cook and be served at the same time, begin with your desired serving time and work backward. Foods with the longest cooking time should be started first, so that all will be ready and hot at the same time.

Safe Food Handling Tips

IN THE KITCHEN

- Wrap raw meat, poultry, and seafood in plastic bags and set on the lowest shelf of the refrigerator to prevent juices from dripping onto other foods. Wash hands thoroughly with soapy water before and after handling raw meat, poultry, and seafood.

- Thoroughly rinse poultry and seafood with cold water and check for any off odors before cooking.

- Wash all utensils, cutting surfaces, and counters with hot, soapy water after contact with raw meat.

- Use a covered, nonmetallic container to marinate meat, poultry, and seafood. Place it in the refrigerator, not on the kitchen counter. Leftover marinade that was in contact with raw meat, poultry, or seafood must be brought to a rolling boil for 1 minute before it is used.

AT THE GRILL

- Never partially cook meat, poultry, or fish and then refrigerate or set aside to finish later.

- Always place grilled food on a clean serving platter and handle with clean utensils. Never use the same unwashed platter that carried the raw meat, poultry, or seafood to the grill for serving the grilled food.

- Do not allow any cooked food to sit out at room temperature for more than 2 hours. Refrigerate cooked foods promptly after serving.

- **All manufacturers of gas and charcoal grills have specific instruction manuals and warnings as to proper use. Please read and follow these instructions carefully.**

Grilling Guide

The following cuts, thicknesses, weights, and grilling times are meant to be guidelines rather than hard and fast rules. Cooking times are affected by such factors as altitude, outside temperature, and desired doneness. Two rules of thumb: Grill steaks, fish fillets, boneless chicken pieces, and vegetables using the Direct Method for the time given on the chart or to desired doneness, turning once halfway through cooking time. Place roasts, whole poultry, whole fish, and thicker cuts in the center of the cooking grate, and grill using the Indirect Method for the time given on the chart, or until an instant-read thermometer registers the desired internal temperature. Cooking times are for medium doneness unless otherwise noted.

Beef

Cut of Meat	Thickness or Weight	Approximate Cooking Time
Steaks: New York, Porterhouse, rib,	1 inch	10-12 minutes
ribeye, T-bone, tenderloin	1½ inches	14–16 minutes
	2 inches	20-25 minutes
Flank steak	1-2 pounds	12-15 minutes
Skirt steak	¼-½ inch	7-9 minutes
Brisket	5-6 pounds	2½-3 hours
Ribeye roast	4-6 pounds	1½-2 hours
Sirloin roast, boneless	4-6 pounds	2-2 ½ hours
Tenderloin roast (rare)	4-5 pounds	50 minutes-1½ hours
Top round roast	4-6 pounds	1¾-2¼ hours
Hamburger	¾ inch	about 10 minutes

Pork

Cut of Meat	Thickness or Weight	Approximate Cooking Time
Chops (rib, loin, shoulder)	¾ inch	12-14 minutes
	1¼-1½ inch	35-40 minutes
Loin blade or sirloin or center rib roast	3-5 pounds	1-2 hours
Rib crown roast	4-6 pounds	1¾-2 hours
Ribs: country-style, back ribs,		
spareribs (well-done)	3-4 pounds	1-1½ hours
Tenderloin	¾-1 pound	25-35 minutes
Top loin roast, double, boneless	3-5 pounds	1½-1¾ hours

Lamb

Cut of Meat	Thickness or Weight	Approximate Cooking Time
Loin and rib chops	1 inch	10-13 minutes
	1½ inch	14-17 minutes
Shoulder and sirloin chops	1 inch	11-14 minutes
	1½ inch	17-19 minutes

Leg of lamb, butterflied	4 pounds	55-65 minutes
Leg roast, boneless, rolled	5-7 pounds	2¼-3 hours
Rib crown roast	3-4 pounds	1¼-1½ hours
Rib roast	2½-3 pounds	1¼-1½ hours

Poultry (well-done)

Type	Thickness or Weight	Approximate Cooking Time
Chicken breasts, skinless, boneless	4-5 ounces	10-12 minutes
Chicken, halves	1¼-1½ pounds	1-1¼ hours
Chicken, whole	3-4 pounds	1¼-1¾ hours
Cornish game hens	1-1½ pounds	45-60 minutes
Turkey, whole, unstuffed	10-12 pounds	2-3 hours
	14-18 pounds	3-4 hours
Turkey drumsticks	½-1½ pounds	¾-1¼ hours

Fish & Seafood

Type	Thickness or Weight	Approximate Cooking Time
Fish fillets	¼-½ inch	3-5 minutes
	½-1 inch	6-10 minutes
Fish steaks	1-1¼ inch	10-12 minutes
Whole fish, unstuffed	1 pound	20-25 minutes
	1½-2 pounds	25-30 minutes
	2-4 pounds	30-50 minutes
Whole fish, stuffed	2 pounds	50-60 minutes
Lobster tails	5 ounces	5-6 minutes
	10 ounces	10-12 minutes
Shrimp, large	1 pound	4-5 minutes

Vegetables

Type	Approximate Cooking Time
Asparagus	7-9 minutes
Baby bok choy	7-9 minutes
Belgian endive	8-10 minutes
Bell peppers, green or red	8-10 minutes
Corn, shucked	10-12 minutes
Eggplant	9-11 minutes
Mushrooms, shiitake or portobello	8-10 minutes
Potatoes (foil wrapped)	50-60 minutes
Squash, patty pan	10-12 minutes
Tomatoes	6-8 minutes
Zucchini, green or yellow	8-10 minutes

Index

Acknowledgments

Weber and the editors wish to thank the following people and organizations for their valuable assistance with this book:

Jack Bittner/Silverado Vineyards; Diane Denoncourt; Martin Francoeur; Lynn Gagné and Michael Burak; Anne Galperin; Fiona Gilsenan; Sara Grynspan; Tom Jakubowski and Barry Goodman/Prop Mart; Bill LeBlond; Marianne Lipanovich; Ian Reeves; Tom Scheibel; Carla and Rich Seidel; Jean Sirois; Michelle Turbide; Becky Wright.